Praise for *Work Miracles*

"We are exposed to so many methods, approaches, ideas and prophets of business success, that the line between results oriented actions, and meaningless motion, is often blurred. Having personally seen the progress an organization can make following the principles and advice contained in Work Miracles, *I recommend it without reservation."*

J.T. Weeker, Area Vice President/Great Lakes Area
United States Postal Service

*"*Work Miracles *does an excellent job of providing practical tools to turn organizational change theories and ideals into action. The 'Transformation Plan' template is particularly powerful as it provides constant visibility to the full nature of our journey as well as tracking our progress toward achieving the future state."*

Carmen West
Manufacturing Technologies Manager,
Inkjet Business Unit, Hewlett-Packard

"This powerful guidebook is an enduring tool to help future leaders build organizations that unlock individual potential and create intentional results. Work Miracles *speaks deeply to the power in all of us to transform our selves and our organizations."*

Carol Pearson, Ph.D.
Best-selling author of *Awakening the Heroes Within* and President of CASA:
The Center for Archetypal Studies and Applications

"The message is clear and powerful. If you want to work miracles then awaken your spirit and take your whole self to work."

Richard Barrett
Fellow of the World Business Academy and Author of
Liberating the Corporate Soul

"There are lots of books about spirit in the workplace, but few translate lofty ideals into practical strategies as well as Work Miracles. *If you are serious about achieving organizational transformation, this book will be an honest and well founded guide to your goal."*

Marsha Willard
Co-author of "Why Teams Can Fail and What to Do About It"

"If you could have only one new tool to advance your organization into the 21st century, Work Miracles *is that tool. The power and possibilities this book can bring to staff and organizations is tremendous."*

Lawrence J. Norvell, President/CPO
United Way of the Columbia-Willamette

"We live in the midst of an ever changing world, which challenges our personal and professional selves. Work Miracles *offers opportunities for self exploration regarding your role in organizational transformation. It creates the road map for the journey all leaders must travel to be effective."*

Kevin W. Sowers, RN, MSN
Senior Associate Chief Operating Officer
Duke University Hospital and Health System

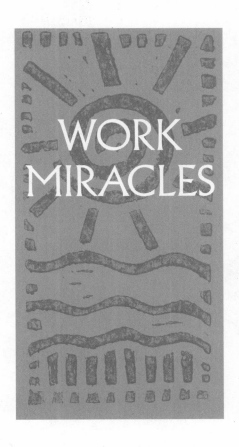

WORK
MIRACLES

WORK MIRACLES:
TRANSFORM YOURSELF AND YOUR ORGANIZATION

Stephen K. Hacker
Marta C. Wilson, Ph.D.

with
Cindy S. Johnston

INSIGHT PRESS™

WORK MIRACLES:
TRANSFORM YOURSELF AND YOUR ORGANIZATION

An Insight Press Book

Library of Congress Catalog Card Number: 99-61591

Printed and bound in the United States of America.

Includes bibliographical references and index

ISBN 0-9667908-0-4 (pbk.)

Insight Press is a trademark of Transformation Systems

Illustrations by: Deb Wildman
Cover Design by: Michele Moldenhauer
Author Photos: Photography by Glenn, Blacksburg

ATTENTION ORGANIZATIONS, ASSOCIATION, AND SCHOOLS: Quantity discounts are available on bulk purchases of this book for educational purposes or fund raising. Book excerpts can also be created to fit specific needs. For information, please contact Insight Press, P.O. Box 1175 Blacksburg, Virginia 24062-1175 or e-mail smithsj@performancecenter.org

To

Robert & Marla

CONTENTS

CONTENTS

CHAPTER 4
CREATE THE CONNECTIONS

CHAPTER 5
ADOPT A DISCIPLINE

A FINAL THOUGHT

APPENDICES

REFERENCES 241

INDEX 246

ABOUT THE AUTHORS 257

FOR FURTHER INFORMATION 259

SPECIAL THANKS

First and foremost, we thank **Cynthia (CJ) Johnston**. We are fortunate that you chose to add your unique voice to this book. Your work demonstrates the power of love and the magic of intention.

John Webb, we credit you with holding up the mirror for us. Your teachings, group interventions, and individual coaching provide an honest look at our personal growth, internal relationships, and overall performance.

Timothy Ludwig, **Bo Hughes**, **Garry Coleman**, and **Altyn Clark**, we are grateful for your personal experiences, contained in many of the sidebars inserted throughout the text.

We thank **Jyl Smithson, Cindy Wilkinson, Jennifer Montgomery, Michele Moldenhauer**, and **Greg Hutchins** for breathing life into the mechanics required to publish our manuscript.

Richard Barrett, Barbara Ryan, **Kenneth Conklin**, **Ray Loog** and **Carolyn Mark**, we appreciate your open, honest, and direct feedback and edits.

For introducing us to excellent change theory and conflict resolution resources, we credit **Ray Butler** and **Floyd Ryan**.

For treasured advice, including the feel of the book, thank you **Elizabeth Holmes Clark** and **Sharon Flinder**.

We recognize **Ted Sienknecht** and **Alexandria Medina** for the initial layout of the text.

We are grateful to **Deborah Randolph Wildman** for the cover artwork and illustrations and to **Susan Bixler** for the book's title.

MORE SPECIAL THANKS

Scott Sink, we appreciate your disciplined pursuit of understanding transformation. Your ongoing work expands the body of knowledge, which we rely upon as a foundation.

We acknowledge **Bob Dryden** for inspirational leadership, bringing forth the best in people, and investing in our work. You continually enable others to live their dreams.

We thank our sponsors, who offer us the opportunity to conduct action research in your organizations. Of particular note, we recognize the knowledge we have gained in the following organizations:

- **U.S. Postal Service**
- **U.S. Geological Survey**
- **U.S. Department of Navy**
- **Loblaws Brands Limited**
- **Kollmorgen Motion Technologies**
- **Botswana National Productivity Centre**
- **Botswana Telecommunications Corporation**

Finally, we are grateful to all sources within our community who have contributed to the creation of this work. Thank you for your energy and insight.

A NOTE TO YOU

Dear Reader ~

Years of discussion gave birth to the idea of a guide for leading transformation. This guide is for people who want to create results in ways that defy apparent possibility. Following, we explore how spiritual consciousness can transform your workplace and offer strategies on how to be, know, do and lead conscious change. We speak with one voice as spiritual partners.

Spirituality is the next frontier for organizations on the quest for performance improvement. The spiritual realm, which is traditionally compartmentalized and separated from the workplace, is now moving towards assimilation. The outcome will be unprecedented performance results at the organizational, group, and individual levels.

The challenge is to raise your consciousness and build a work environment that allows this spiritual potential to grow. In *Work Miracles*, we explore how you can choose a creation stance and then, in concert with others, form a vision community with unlimited potential. Our message is simple. First, become self aware. While continuing to care for yourself, give your relationships the attention they need. With this foundation established, learn and implement a comprehensive, integrated and strategic methodology for leading organizational transformation.

Developing a creation community within an organization is complex because it requires breakthrough or transformational change. Barriers within and among individuals must be surfaced, explored, and addressed. When this does not happen, the workplace often becomes a stage where the dramas of fear, intimidation, sabotage, blame and control play out as actors perform unconscious scripts.

Workplace community begins when people become aware of these unhealthy patterns of thinking and behaving and collectively release them. A web of potential change is then woven, its strands being conscious individuals and honest relationships. If you have the desire to face obstacles that prevent you from unlocking your full potential and creating such a community, this book is for you.

You can facilitate the growth of a more conscious, nimble and effective organization. It requires enrolling others to get involved in their own evolution, the quality of their relationships, and the vision of their organization. It also includes enrolling them in you.

We work with many organizations large and small, public and private, progressive and conservative. In all these settings, leaders struggle to get others to embrace the passion and creative tension that accompany improvement. Nevertheless, they are successful.

Throughout this book, we weave stories of real struggles with strategies for achieving organizational, group and individual transformations. We find it impossible to separate these three types of improvement. Perhaps this is as it should be, given that transformation occurs on many levels.

Writing this book has changed our lives forever. We hope it enriches your spiritual journey and inspires an abundance of work miracles in your life.

Warmest wishes ~

Marta & Stephen

OVERVIEW
What You Will Find In This Book

A miracle is an event that seems impossible to be explained by natural laws, so it is regarded as supernatural in origin. When we are united with each other and our spiritual source, miracles happen. In this book, we discuss how members of work communities can consciously unlock and align their energies and create miracles. We call such phenomena *work miracles*. Work miracles has two meanings, depending on whether work is used as a noun or verb. We use both meanings throughout the book.

This book's five chapters contain discoveries about work miracles:

- Chapter 1 ~ Awaken Your Spirit
- Chapter 2 ~ Expand Your Potential
- Chapter 3 ~ Lead with Energy
- Chapter 4 ~ Create the Connections
- Chapter 5 ~ Adopt a Discipline

CHAPTER 1
EXPLORES SPIRITUALITY AT WORK

Spirit in the Workplace

Work settings today are filled with people who contain shiny diamonds. Unfortunately for many people, clutter has accumulated around their diamonds. This residue hides their purest essence from most other people who meet and know them. However, diamonds in the rough are completely capable of removing their clutter and adopting a way of being that repels a repeated buildup of residue in the future. Self-awareness is a polishing process that can uncover your diamond. When a critical mass within an organization undertakes this challenge, it creates brilliance beyond compare and sets the stage for transformation.

All organizations are rich with hidden energy

Work settings are filled with people whose inner diamonds are brilliant but their potential is untapped

Transformation Cornerstones

Four essential cornerstones must underlie any successful organizational transformation or improvement initiative. Together, these transformation cornerstones provide a framework in which to create alignment and sustainable breakthrough improvement: 1) Self Awareness; 2) Interpersonal Insight; 3) Requirements for Success; and 4) Change Mechanisms.

In a nutshell, find people who have the energy to do what needs to be done and give them the tools to craft their own evolution. Give them the skills to improve themselves and their relationships in a way that is meaningful and inspirational. And, integrate tried and true methods for strategic planning and defining requirements for success into a comprehensive approach to organizational change.

CHAPTER 2
EXPLORES SELF AWARENESS

Johari's Window

In order to know yourself better, it helps if you collect as much information as possible from those around you. The use of Johari's Window allows your friends, family, and associates to help you evaluate what you do not know about yourself.

Being, Doing, and Having

Self awareness requires getting in touch with being, doing and having. Being is aliveness and consciousness. Doing is action and directed energy. Having is coexisting with things and people around you. Each one supports the other two.

The Power of Intention
The results you create are an absolute function of intention. Intention underlies all personal and organizational transformation. Change mechanisms are just tools and not the key leverage point. Intention has a 100 percent relationship to whether or not results are achieved. Related to the power of intention are 1) choice, 2) risk taking and effectiveness, 3) attitude, and 4) mental stance.

Personal Blueprint
The process of setting direction and goals facilitates the creation of what you want in life. You can then sharpen your life's direction and change your goals as often as needed. Goals give you a clear focal point on which to direct your natural creativity. In the context of personal mastery, goals serve as a path toward inspiration and creation. Two tools that can help shape your personal blueprint are the Individual Development Document and the Life Plan.

Levels of Effectiveness
You create a comfort zone when in mystery. Staying in your comfort zone is easy and requires taking a risk in order to break free of it. You must gain clear intention in order to take the risk. Once the risk is taken, you can gain insight and experience breakthroughs by carefully observing your performance. Following repeated practice and feedback, you have the opportunity to increase your effectiveness. Then, the process starts all over again if you choose to move to a higher level of effectiveness.

CHAPTER 3
EXPLORES VISION ALIGNMENT

Traditional Alignment

The outcome of a traditional alignment session is the conscious or the unconscious bending of personal "arrows" into compliance with the organizational vision. In some cases, it can result in the momentary formation of a personal vision where none existed before.

Vision Community Alignment

When individual energy lines become defined, you can assess what the organization has the energy to accomplish. Individuals become clear on personal vision and then discover how closely it is aligned with the organization's vision. This clarity of direction produces more energy for the organization than manipulative force could ever generate.

Vision Alignment Process

Step 1: Develop collective consciousness of personal visions.

Step 2: Define organizational requirements for success.

Step 3: Declare energy interests.

Step 4: Ensure there is sufficient energy to achieve organizational requirements.

CHAPTER 4
EXPLORES RELATIONSHIPS

Interpersonal Insight
Interpersonal insight includes the capacity to appropriately discern and respond to other people's moods, temperaments, motivations, and desires. This is done through leadership, social analysis, relationship management and conflict resolution.

Work Rules
Relationship management can be greatly improved through the use of ground rules, which have proven to create rapid and sustainable results in the areas of personal effectiveness, relationship management, and organizational performance. Because of their direct application to the work environment, we refer to them as "work rules." Work rules are principle-centered guidelines for building interpersonal insight and high-performance relationships.

Feedback and Trust
Feedback is a great way to increase self-awareness by seeking honest observations from other people. Seeking feedback can help build trust. Trust is a foundational element of relationship management. Another way to build trust is the Trust Exercise. Similar to the Feedback Exercise, it involves sharing honest observations and reveals how others perceive us in areas that otherwise would not be shared.

Conflict Resolution

Masters of interpersonal relations are frequently excellent mediators who prevent conflicts or resolve those that flare up. Mediation is one of the most difficult elements of interpersonal mastery because people are reluctant to deal with conflict. Conflict resolution requires hard work and perseverance. The key is to move beyond conflict and to channel spiritual energy into the co-creation of results.

CHAPTER 5
EXPLORES MANAGING CHANGE

Creation vs. Reaction

Reaction and creation are polar opposites, and occur at both the individual and organizational levels. It is difficult but necessary to move individuals and whole organizations from reaction to creation.

Transformation Cycle

The Transformation Cycle includes traditional components of strategic planning, such as assessing and diagnosing the organization, defining a mission and vision, and identifying improvement objectives. Additionally, this large-scale transformation approach focuses on building commitment to the plan, managing implementation, aligning individuals and teams toward common objectives, and creating community to make the plan happen.

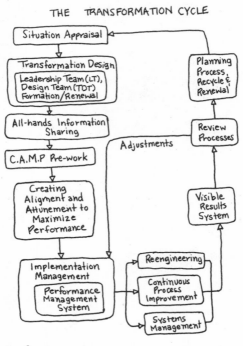

THE TRANSFORMATION CYCLE

Transformation Plan

    The Transformation Plan visibly represents the present state and desired future state as well as how to close the gap between the two.

PAST	PRESENT	PATH			FUTURE	
	Point of Departure	Drivers & Enablers	12 1 2 3 4 5 6 7 8 9 10 11	RESULT	12 - month point of arrival	VISION
Encores						
~~						
~~						
~~						
Never Agains						
~~						
~~						
~~						
Release Baggage	What's Working? What's Not working?	INSTRUMENT PANEL				
Carry Forward Lessons Learned						

Chapter 1

AWAKEN YOUR SPIRIT

"And whatever else high performance and excellence may be based on, they would seem to have something to do with the quality of Spirit... human Spirit, our Spirit, the Spirit of our organizations."

- Terrence Deal and Pamela Hawkins

Spirit in Latin means breath, which symbolizes life and the essence of being. Spirit compels us to seek transformational experiences. It motivates us to understand the unknown. It helps us define our purpose. It shapes the work we do. In this book, we explore the rich role that spirit can play in your workplace. Questions addressed include:

- Can you make the workplace more meaningful?
- Do you see evidence of your coworkers' spirits?
- Can you introduce spirituality into the workplace?
- How do you show up to carry out your day-to-day routine?
- Do you display your spirit at work, or do you reserve it for off-hours?
- What is the cost to the organization of showing up as partial beings in the workplace?

The workplace of the past was alive with spirit. The agrarian lifestyle tied together all aspects of the farmer's existence: family, community, personal growth, vocation, finances, and bodily sustenance. These dimensions merged to define the person, representing the farmer's spiritual expression.

Although it was a difficult life, the connection to the land was often expressed in spiritual terms. The passing from generation to generation of how to work and be one with the land was as important as the seed of life itself. In today's post-industrial age, this type of balanced lifestyle is rare.

Today, compartmentalization of life has fragmented the individual. There is little integration of interests and activities. Instead, people strive to solve a complex equation that often appears to have no solution.

For many, family responsibilities compete with work duties. No time remains for personal reflection. The hustle to complete activities replaces work harmony. The hope that these activities will magically add up to a larger meaning is lost.

Balancing family, spirit, vocation and other dimensions requires individuals, groups and organizations to transform. This transformation, or renewal, can only occur after intense personal and interpersonal examination. This examination facilitates attainment of a heightened spiritual state within and among individuals.

Individuals who experience this heightened state of consciousness create a groundswell of spiritual community within the work environment. Read on to discover how to build community and bring spirit back into the workplace.

Everybody has a transformation story, whether they can see it or not. I volunteered to talk about mine because I view this experience as a step that will move me forward in my transformation. I'm not sure what I'm going to say. I acknowledge myself for taking the risk and for overcoming my fear of judgment.

RELEASE A LIFE SPRING OF ENERGY

Today more than ever, we see the need to revive the spirit of organizations — to release a life spring of untapped energy. This spirit is transcendental, weaving itself throughout our hearts and minds. It:

- compels us to search beyond our human limitations;
- moves us beyond failure toward new attitudes, goals and accomplishments;
- draws us closer together; and
- directs us toward common purpose and meaning.

The Relevance of Spirituality

We now live in a world where technology, efficiency, and productivity have become workplace mantras. This leaves little room for matters of the spirit. Managers often, consciously or otherwise, seek to sterilize today's organizations — to deaden spirit rather than to encourage it.

Some people ask if spirituality even has a place at work. Many believe that spirituality falls strictly within the domain of religious institutions. They do not see that spirituality has relevance within the organizational context. We believe differently.

People cannot be separated from their essential natures. Theologian John Wagner (1988) writes:

> *"If spirituality is understood as having to do with fundamental matters, with our lives at their deepest, with what counts most for us, it cannot be segregated from any aspect of our existence. It has to*

*do with our solitude and our corporate life. It has
to do with the way we think and feel and act in
every circumstance. It has to do with the whole of
our lives, our public selves as well."*

Nurture the Spirit

In the absence of nurturing peoples' spirits, an organization of individuals is no more than a body of broken bones.
Awakening individual spirit is essential to the development of
any organizational transformation. In fact, we believe the car-
dinal element of failed organizational transformation efforts is
a limited understanding of the relationship between spiritual
health and work performance.

Many organizations have improved their technical and
operational systems while relationships have languished. This
is a fatal flaw of many organizations whose leaders believe that
information and technology will fundamentally change the way
people work, relate, and improve performance. Why has this
happened? Many organizations have forgotten to nurture the
spirits of their most important resource, people. In the following sections we discuss what is involved in awakening the spirit
of individuals in the workplace.

SPIRITUALITY AT WORK

We believe that all reality is spiritual. Our line of thought
is inclusive of many theologies. We are concerned with the
subject of spirituality, not particular religions, which represent
different paths toward spirituality. We honor all these paths as
we discuss spirituality in the workplace.

5

Connect to the Source

Spirit is both within and around us. An aspect of spirituality is how people connect with each other and to the universal source of energy. When we are spiritually weak, we are separated from this source and estranged from the force of collective spirits. We are weak because we are on our own, isolated.

We believe most people desire a stronger connection to their source. Some people have a clearer vision of their desired connection than others. In any case, if you take time to compare your current connection to your desired connection, you are likely to sense a gap between where you are and where you want to be. This gap produces creative spiritual tension.

Like the tension of a stretched rubber band, a strong and clear vision can pull you toward your desired state and help you overcome barriers along the way. The clearer your vision, the more creative spiritual tension you have. This tension is energy. If properly channeled, it can work miracles.

Work Miracles

A miracle is defined as an event that seems impossible to explain by natural laws and so is regarded as supernatural in origin. When we are united with each other and our spiritual source, our output is divine. We can work miracles.

In the workplace when we are spiritually deprived, we find ourselves connected to nothing bigger than work. Thus, feelings of insignificance, weakness, and despair can emerge. On the other hand, when we are connected to the larger river of spiritual energy, we are able to accomplish more.

A central characteristic of spirituality is the desire to go beyond your self interests — to make a difference in creating a more meaningful world. Spirituality is living and breathing by your inner truth to produce positive attitudes and relationships in your life. This individual desire to make a positive difference is essential to building community at work, since community springs from the individual intentions of all who populate the workplace.

In building a community, individuals experience a radical transformation and awakening when deeply embedded attitudes and actions are examined, challenged, and changed. Spirits awaken. Only then can individuals transform. Only then will committed individuals form a creation community.

Easy to Recognize, Impossible to Define

What does this all mean? Performance improvement efforts will go nowhere without vision and spirit. Leaders must create a collective vision with which people are willing to align themselves. This can be a team, plant, business unit, or company vision.

Dee Hock (1983), the former head of VISA, distilled it when he said:

> *"In the field of group endeavor, you will see incredible events in which the group performs far beyond the sum of its individual talents. It happens in the symphony, in the ballet, in the theater, in sports, and equally in business. It is easy to recognize and*

impossible to define. It is a mystique. It cannot be achieved without immense effort, training and co-operation. But training and cooperation alone rarely create it."

The mystical "it" that Hock credits for virtuoso performance is the spiritual essence of culture. Many have seen this effect.

After an extensive study of teams, Peter Vaill (1989) concluded that spirit was at the core of every successful group. Group members felt that spirit was essential to the value and meaning of the group's work. Culture, not command and control, propelled successful groups toward their destinies.

The discovery (or re-discovery) of the value of spirit in the workplace is in vogue. What has recently occurred to make workplace spirituality significant for all of us? And what originally caused spirituality to disappear from the workplace? Let us look at history.

A BRIEF HISTORY OF WORK

Written history chronicles our last five thousand years or so. Ancient artifacts cover at least half a million more years of our existence. All these records suggest that our survival instinct has preserved us.

In The Beginning

Since the dawn of history, humankind created things. The tools we made during the Stone Age illustrate our creative mind. We fabricated weapons to procure food and combat

enemies. These were products of human skill and workman-
ship. From many sites in every part of the world, archeologists
have collected millions of artifacts which reveal the character
and life of the people who made them.

When a behemoth charged, our survival instinct taught
us to get out of the way. Protecting ourselves against preda-
tors, we learned quickly to adapt to our environment or perish.
This survival instinct caused us to hunt and forage for food
using all of our developing senses and knowledge.

The homo sapien mind was constantly seeking to control the elements while securing a future for the species through
the family unit. Primarily through the family, knowledge was
passed on to descendants. In this way, wisdom and beliefs were
transmitted from one generation to another, laying a foundation for modern culture.

Prehistoric people addressed the "meaning of it all"
through constructing myths and spiritual beliefs. They did not
divide life into fragments. Instead, they saw the necessity of
the whole person showing up in every instance. Humankind
survived and advanced by integrating body, mind, and spirit.

The Basics

As we became more capable of obtaining life's essen-
tials, we began to express our spirituality more pointedly. An
example can be found in Egyptian history. Between 5000 BC
and 3100 BC, the people of Egypt were nomadic hunters and
food gatherers, heavily occupied with basic survival.

Then, they discovered the power of the rich river delta.
Its soil provided agricultural potential. Using this potential,

9

the Egyptians developed the capacity to go beyond daily biological needs, food and shelter. They employed this extra societal energy to express a collective spirituality in building many great architectural treasures.

Another profound change occurred when people began to organize beyond the family and clan. It started with the formation of armies, kingdoms, and religious institutions. This type of organization called for more specialization instead of development of the whole individual.

Rising from the great empires of Rome and Greece, the European System evolved during the Renaissance Period. At the same time, industrialization began to take place in Italy. Then in the early 1700s, the era of manufacturing began in the British Isles.

Man as Machine

The scientific mind generated ideas to manufacture machines that could produce machines. Development of the modern lathe around 1800 contributed to the American system of manufacturing.

Eli Whitney, the inventor of the cotton gin, promoted manufacturing with interchangeable parts. Whitney used jigs and fixtures to orient and hold parts, which could be made by less-skilled machinists. Factories adopted this manufacturing system which treated and used people as machines. The ability to think was not believed to add much value. The use of a person as a tool for manufacturing simply required the human machine to show up at work.

Frederick Taylor's methods contributed to a more efficient use of human energy in manufacturing. Industry used Taylor's techniques to make manufacturing systems more productive. Rampant cynicism developed around the fact that people were seen simply as cogs in a large machine.

Fragmentation of the human being had occurred inside the workplace, in the arts, in educational institutions, and in the family. People brought to the workplace only what was required of them at the time. Then came war.

Out of Ashes

From the ashes of World War II, we rediscovered the worth of the human spirit, and the genius each person possesses. The Japanese post-war development was envied by all. Their approach allowed thinking employees to drive toward perfection as individuals and within teams.

The complete rebuilding of Germany and its technologically renovated factories provided additional evidence of the strength of the human mind and spirit. Valuable knowledge was gained by investigating how countries ravaged by war could rebuild to compete and win.

Many American organizations were not up to the challenge. American industry panicked and began to invite its workers to think again. No longer was punching a clock acceptable. Employees were asked to contribute their total capabilities. The presence of the active mind was at first encouraged and later required.

Tremendous social shifts occurred when technical problem solving became obligatory, often within a team setting.

Semi-conductors again changed the world of business and ac-celerated invention. Workplace re-engineering and employee retraining were required, with special emphasis on creativity and problem solving. And now, due to the interrelationship between creativity and spirit, the seemingly stronger subject of spirituality is being entertained by business.

Full Circle

Creation is a manifestation of the spirit. Spirit, both individual and collective, is a prerequisite to the creation process. Now the workplace has come full circle. Once again the whole human (body, mind and spirit) is required for work to thrive and prosper.

Are we at a major crossroads again? The advancing technological pace has focused attention on the importance of business competition and the critical contributions of employees. Without engaging the great force of our individual and collective spirituality, organizations cannot move forward. What then, can be done to expose, nurture, and reinforce organizational spirit? What attributes do creation communities seem to share?

CREATION AT WORK

To frame our approach, we introduce several key concepts. This is not an exhaustive list, but rather key elements meant to aid in developing a mindset for spiritual growth.

As you read on, prepare yourself for some surprises. Get ready to reconsider the role of leadership, the meaning of evolution, the relevance of expression, the value of play, the importance of beauty, the dignity of choice, and the power of love.

Leaders of Spirit

Anyone and everyone can become a leader of his or her own spiritual journey. This is where leadership starts. Leadership is a spiritual activity. However, a spiritual leader does not have to be someone with hierarchical power or authority. We discuss leadership as a spiritual activity in Chapter 3.

The common feature of spiritual leaders is they find themselves in the humbling position of seeking to understand the wholeness, gifts, and hearts of others. They recognize and empower the talent within and around them. They do this in order to weave a unified cultural tapestry.

Sally Helgesen (1995) cites many examples of such weaving in her book *The Web of Inclusion*. A web is natural and organic, not modeled on a machine. Like a spider's web, a "web of inclusion" is both a structure and an ever-evolving process, constantly changing to meet the demands of the business environment.

Building a "web of inclusion" involves:
* employee participation
* talents, not titles
* flexibility
* strategic alliances

First, ideas are solicited from all employees, not just imposed from the top down. Second, what individuals do in the workplace depends on their talents, not on their titles. Third, a premium is placed on flexibility. Fourth, the edges of the web connect with people outside the organization such as customers, suppliers, joint-venture partners, and the media.

For leaders who are intent upon building a "web of inclusion," loyalty and fairness have equal merit to productivity, accountability, and diversity. More importantly, this quality of commitment is known throughout the culture. Leaders of spirit create a nourishing environment in which people are encouraged to explore their unique being, connect with others, and develop a powerfully moving and energizing collective story.

Leadership becomes an essential ingredient for awakening the spirit of people, for nurturing transformation, and for growing authentic creation communities.

Release Your Diamond

Spiritual awakening within the workplace assumes maturity, growth and evolution of its individuals. One might compare individuals to diamonds: precious, shining, and beautiful inside. At the moment of birth, we are full of light.

Each of us comes into the world fresh, dazzling, and pure. Throughout our lives, many of us lose our luster, attracting a dull build-up of clutter. Still, we are precious, shining and beautiful inside.

In order to release the beauty of diamonds, they are extracted from surrounding bedrock and then cut to release their inner beauty and brightness. People can have a similar experience.

Work settings today are filled with people who contain shiny diamonds. These people once naturally and freely sought and experienced knowledge of the world around them, joy in their interactions, and beauty in their environment.

Unfortunately for many people, clutter in the form of disappointments, punishment, pressure to conform, discouragement, harbored guilt, and repressed anger has accumulated around their diamonds. This residue hides their purest essence from most other people who meet and know them.

Dull and frustrated, individuals find it difficult to tap into their own energy, motivation, and passion. However, these diamonds in the rough are completely capable of removing their clutter and adopting a way of being that repels a repeated buildup of residue in the future.

Cleaning many years of accumulated buildup exposes the lustrous facets of our diamonds. However, chipping away the old residue is no small task. This process demands knowledge, dedication, care, discipline, and perseverance. We are each responsible for our own polishing process. With some basic tools and approaches, we all have the ability to remove the tarnish and residue.

Some individuals will seize the opportunity for heightened awareness through facilitated self-exploration, and they will take charge of their personal mastery process. Others will resist. We do not recommend that anyone be forced to take on the challenge of personal change. We do recommend that individuals be given time and flexibility to explore their worldview and to understand themselves better. When the student is ready, the teacher will appear.

Taking charge of your personal discovery process is what we call spiritual evolution. It is a polishing process that can uncover your diamond. When a critical mass within an organization undertakes this challenge, it creates brilliance beyond compare.

All organizations are rich with
hidden energy

Work settings are filled with people
whose inner diamonds are brilliant
but their potential is untapped

Figure 1: The Inner Diamond

I was a late bloomer. I didn't recognize the importance of being spiritually centered until my late twenties. I didn't act on the realization until my mid-thirties. But I can honestly say to anyone that it doesn't matter where you are or how old you are. It's never too late to start. And here's another thing I've learned, you don't just get it one day and ride the wave. It's a continual process of renewal. It's a fragile thing. The world isn't set up right now in a way that reinforces the spirit, so you have to do a lot of the care and feeding yourself.

Expression

Expressive activity liberates the spirit. For example, in *Boiling Energy*, Richard Katz (1982) describes the healing dance of the !Kung, a tribe in the Kalahari Desert on the northwestern edge of Botswana (a country in which we have worked for several years):

> *"Four times a month on the average, night signals the start of a healing dance. The women sit around the fire rhythmically clapping. The men, sometimes joined by the women, dance around the singers. As the dance intensifies, NUM, or spiritual energy, is*

*activated in the healers, but mostly among the danc-
ing men. As NUM is activated in them, they begin to KIA, or experience enhancement of their consciousness. While experiencing KIA, they heal all
those at the dance. Before the sun rises fully the
next morning, the dance usually ends. Those at the
dance find it exciting, joyful, powerful. 'Being at a
dance makes our hearts happy,' the !Kung say."*

Spirit is released or transformed by people engaged together in meaningful, expressive activity. For the !Kung, the
primary source of spiritual energy is created by their dances.
Just as the !Kung find their spiritual center in the healing dance,
people in many organizations find their spiritual center in myth,
ritual, ceremony, stories, and acts of creation.

How do these expressive activities liberate our spirit?
To answer the question, think of a time when you were particularly swayed or uplifted. Almost always the exhilaration of
spirit was a response to something expressive such as a work of
art, a song, a poem, a moving ceremony, a meaningful ritual,
or a well-told story.

People who form creation communities institutionalize
the acceptance and appreciation of expressive actions within
the workplace and implement ways to celebrate these activities. For instance, there is play.

Play — The Natural Gift of A Child
Another component in awakening organizational spirituality is to relearn how to play, the natural gift of the child.

Play seems to be conspicuously absent from society. The natural gaiety and laughter of the child within us is lost in proportion to the loss of our ability to play.

It is fascinating to observe the many contexts in which the word "play" is used. We use it unconsciously without any thought of its fundamental meaning. The word often loses its connection with natural joy.

As described by Helen Luke (1995) in her book *The Way of Woman*, every dramatic performance is called play. All actors are players as well as all musicians, sports enthusiasts, and game players. Tragedy, comedy, and music are all performed by players. Some players appreciate and understand the nature of play and convey its joy to audiences.

But there are many people who have no perception of the meaning of play in today's workforce. They want to acquire fame, money or self-satisfaction by sensational performances, often without meaning. This is the opposite of play.

Think about the importance of true recreation (re-CREATION). Until joy, laughter, and play for the sake of creation wholly infuse our lives, we are not truly alive. In this scenario, work and play are no longer separate activities but instead are fully integrated.

People are fully realized and totally involved and committed when they are at play. Talking about what truly brings joy to human spirit, Joseph Campbell (1988) writes:

> *"If you have the guts to follow the risk, however, life opens, opens, opens up along the line. I'm not superstitious, but I do believe in spiritual magic,*

you might say. I feel that if one follows what I call one's 'bliss' — the thing that really gets you deep in the gut and that you feel in your life — doors will open up. They do! They have in my life and they have in many lives that I know of."

The Experience of Beauty

Appreciation for and creation of beauty in the workplace is food for the spirit. In our work, many of us have forgotten how to cherish and revere beauty. We have allowed beauty to sink into a deep slumber from which she may not return. The kiss of the mythical prince can take the simple form of appreciating beauty in others and cherishing what they create.

If we take time to look, we can see peoples' beauty manifest itself in many ways. For example, we can find it in their writing, organizing, theorizing, challenging, teaching, and serving to name a few. The more we look for beauty, the more we see it. A leader of spirit brings this principle alive within the organizational culture.

The setting in which people constantly seek to find each other's beauty is also very special and delicate. Small miracles manifest daily in such a place. Work is more pleasing.

Plants, drawings, and sculptures appear. Clothes look better. Looking around, the glow of health is visible. People take care of themselves and support others. They live life as an art. They embrace and exercise the power of choice.

The Power of Choice

Another aspect of awakening spirituality is the realization that there are various approaches to living. How we live our lives is a mental choice. In making this choice, you determine a lot about how your life plays out.

One approach to life is that we drift from one event to another, without a sense of direction or purpose, somewhat like being on a drifting raft sometimes feeling like victims, sometimes feeling lucky. Or it may even seem as if life is a series of reactions.

In this reality, we live our lives through our problems, pain, frustrations, and feelings of being a victim. We call this stance being "at effect," which means being at the mercy of life's daily happenings and hoping that life will deliver good experiences and material gains to our door.

In contrast, we can also choose to build, explore, and create. We can choose to see our connection to all that surrounds us. We call this being "at cause," which means taking charge of the process of our lives.

At this point, we simply ask the question "Do we have any choice in how we spend our lives?" Our answer is, "Absolutely yes, we have the possibility of choice."

But if we do not know how to use our choices, words of encouragement will not aid us. Likewise, if people in an organization do not know how to use choice when leadership offers it, few if any gains will be made.

Therefore, the leader of spirit must become a student of choice. A starting point is to recognize that attitude itself is a choice. How we think about something is instrumental in determining the choices available to us.

I was in a rut. It was time for a change.
Here was my average day:

Get up.
Eat breakfast.
Shower.
Dress.
Go to work.
Work.
Come home.
Eat dinner.
Feed cat.
Exercise.
Read.
Talk on phone.
Read some more.
Go to bed.
Sleep.

So I created something different for myself. A truly exciting life filled with energy and passion. Now a typical day looks like this:

Get up!!!!!

Eat BREAKFAST!! Shower!!!!!

Dress!!!!!

GO TO WORK!!! Work!

Come home!

Eat dinner!!!!!

Feed Cat!!!!!

Exercise!

Read!!!

Talk on phone!!!!!

READ SOME MORE!!!!!

Go to bed!!!!!

Sleep!!!!

There is much to know about selecting a mental stance, exercising choice, and organizing your life to create desired results. This knowledge is not in the realm of absolute truth. Instead, it lies in your reality as you interact with the world.

Leaders of creation communities help individuals see the need to expand their knowledge of mental stances and choice through modeling and being the example. This is a foundational element for awakening and nurturing spirituality. Choice is ultimately a necessary building block for a creation community.

In a true community we respect diversity; and thus, we do not propose unwilling conversion to the acceptance of choice. Instead, we suggest putting principles into practice that allow people to understand the power of choice and to use it within the workplace. A creation community puts no limits on human potential.

An environment in which individuals see and have the power of choice contains unlimited possibilities. Each of us has the power to be a carrier of knowledge, wisdom and inspiration. The choice is truly ours.

The Foundation of Love

Finally, it is difficult to awaken workplace spirituality without acknowledging love and peace as cornerstones. However difficult, we discuss these concepts openly and keep them visible during the lifetime of a creation community.

Peace is much more than the absence of unhealthy conflict. It is a condition unto itself. There is more to being healthy than the absence of illness, and there is more to peace than the absence of hostility.

In today's workplace, our goal must be creation of peace. Without love, there is no peace. Where love is absent at work, unhealthy conflict is inevitable.

We realize a commitment to love is disruptive to today's organizations. Unhealthy conflict does not threaten the status quo, in many ways it bolsters it. Love is a threat to the established order. Love changes things. It breaks down barriers.

Mentally, we have exiled love. We have segregated it to narrow regions of social dialogue. Love is considered an acceptable conversation between lovers, but not among coworkers. It is fascinating that our emotional development has not kept pace with our material progress. Our modes of thinking have fallen behind our technologies.

A creation community is a collection of healing, caring, and loving individuals who build and sustain a culture founded on bringing into being that which did not exist before. We would not dream of using outmoded building techniques to construct a bridge, but our mental techniques are obsolete for designing and developing creation communities. We can send people into space, but we cannot sustain civility in the workplace. That is because the latter task demands heart (Williamson, 1994).

A creation community thrives with a strong heart. It crumbles if it is weak. Its foundation must be built upon solid cornerstones.

FOUR TRANSFORMATION CORNERSTONES

So how do you instill the value of expression, play, beauty, choice and love in your organization? Over the past few years we have worked with organizations worldwide. In these settings, leaders have struggled with understanding and adapting to change. These leaders struggled to enroll people in improvement initiatives, especially when there was no immediate or apparent crisis.

We believe that four essential cornerstones must underlie any organizational transformation or improvement initiative:

- Self Awareness - individuals must pursue and achieve personal and professional mastery;
- Interpersonal Insight - relationships must be managed and nurtured to foster interpersonal growth;
- Requirements for Success - the value exchange must be clarified and understood; and
- Change Mechanisms - appropriate methods to drive and enable organizational transformation must be shared and implemented.

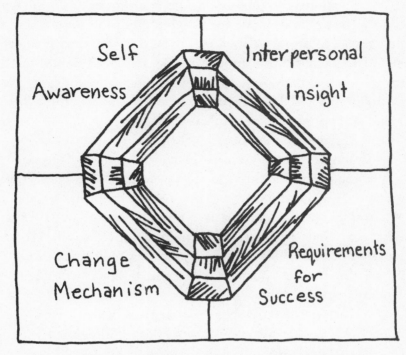

Self Awareness

Interpersonal Insight

Change Mechanism

Requirements for Success

Together, these four cornerstones can help release the untapped potential in your organization.

Figure 2: The Four Transformation Cornerstones

This means you must find people who have the energy to do what needs to be done and give them the tools to craft their own evolution. Give them the skills to improve themselves and their relationships in a way that is meaningful and inspirational. Finally, integrate tried and true methods for strategic planning and defining requirements for success into a comprehensive approach to organizational change.

Together, these four transformation cornerstones provide leaders with a framework in which to create alignment and sustainable breakthrough improvement. We believe that integrated organizational transformation, community building, and strategic planning initiatives must build upon these cornerstones. Such initiatives become more effective than those that are not built upon these cornerstones. You can eliminate the isolation of single-purpose approaches by addressing all these elements concurrently.

Our experience is that necessary business change is also more effective when all four cornerstones are integrated as part of a comprehensive long-term improvement strategy. Let's take a look at each transformation cornerstone.

Self Awareness

In self awareness we:

- break down our own barriers;
- seek feedback;
- release our past baggage;
- understand and expand our innate potential;
- explore what we do not know about ourselves;

- define our contribution and commitment;
- pay the price of making a contribution;
- clarify our intentions;
- examine our mental stance;
- take risks that increase our levels of knowledge; and
- create positive and sustainable behavior changes.

Self awareness involves raising our level of consciousness about ourselves and our vocation. It is a choice. Some people choose the path of self awareness when confronting a crisis or a significant life event such as divorce, death, or downsizing. Others take the path of avoiding immediate pain or discomfort and move towards unconsciousness, a deep rut that further clouds the brilliance of their diamond.

Why might many choose not to explore deeper levels? It may be that they quake at the awesome power within, not at facing their weaknesses. Nelson Mandela (1994) stated,

"Our deepest fear is that we are powerful beyond measure. It is our light, not our darkness that most frightens us. We ask ourselves, who am I to be brilliant, gorgeous, talented, and fabulous? Actually, who are you not to be? You are a child of God."

The Process of Self Awareness
Components of this process we have identified and found useful for individuals to create include:

29

- the release of fear;
- personal vision;
- purpose and mission statements;
- personal values and operating principles;
- conditions for success and joyful experiences;
- role definitions;
- point of departure (current state and self-image);
- point of arrival (desired future state and self-image);
- action plans to close effectiveness gaps;
- style preferences;
- perceived roadblocks;
- strategies to get around roadblocks; and
- enhancing strengths and minimizing weaknesses.

You may notice the similarity of these components to those of strategic planning. In essence, this process is a personal strategic planning process. We have incorporated these components into templates and exercises that make sense and help create a Life Plan.

An early step in developing spiritual community in the workplace is to assist key people in their self awareness process and to check alignment of their personal vision with the organizational vision. Our experience ties the most successful transformation initiatives to leaders who are committed to their own self awareness and to assisting others in the same process.

Interpersonal Insight

Beyond self awareness, we grow and develop through our interactions with people. Interpersonal growth requires interpersonal insight. Interpersonal insight is related to social intelligence, which we discuss in more detail in Chapter 4. An examination of the varied types of organizations in the world today teaches us that poor relationships within organizations are the primary drivers of performance problems.

Yet few change initiatives attempt to address these interpersonal tensions directly and constructively. As more organizations adopt team-based approaches to improvement, we are called upon to manage a significant number of relationships in a more meaningful and productive way than ever before.

There are many facets to interpersonal insight and many ways to customize interventions in areas such as:

- creative conflict resolution;
- high-performance work systems;
- group dynamics;
- organizational behavior; and
- human resource systems.

Three of the most powerful approaches to interpersonal insight are among the simplest. We must manage:

- agreements;
- trust; and
- feedback.

We explore each of these in Chapter 4. Along with self awareness, interpersonal insight is a crucial cornerstone of organizational transformation. The third transformation cornerstone is requirements for success.

Requirements for Success

For your group or organization to work miracles, the requirements for success need to be fully captured. The fact that people in your organization create agreement with people in other organizations calls into question, "What is the value exchange?" By value exchange we mean the basis upon which two entities form a relationship.

Why are your organization's customers and suppliers in relationship with you? What is the value derived by each party? Understanding the nature of value exchanges created between organizations and their individuals is important, given that these relationships are generally elective by nature. Organizations embracing the perspective of value exchange operate on a different playing field from the majority.

These organizations see forming and growing relationships between themselves and other groups as a keystone to value exchange. They do not limit performance evaluation to simple comparisons with last year's financial figures or with their direct competitor's commercial performance.

They also measure:
- the health of external relationships;
- quality of their products and services;
- responsiveness to market changes;
- time to market of new products and services;
- customer satisfaction on an array of criteria; and

- performance of the development process for products, services, and relationships.

Current relationships are defined in terms of present and full-potential value exchange, and the organization moves to close the gap between the two.

At the most basic level, value from customer relationships can be increased in three ways. The first is to acquire new customers. The second is to motivate existing customers to engage in behaviors that generate higher returns. The third, if the value exchange is high, is to extend the duration of the customer relationship in order to maintain the desired behaviors over a longer time.

The models that drive most organizational decisions do not focus on this third point. Questions to ask yourself about the value exchange include:

- Upon what foundation are current customer relationships built...what is the value exchange?
- What percentage does my organization currently have of potential or target customers...how many could it have?
- Why do customers seek to be in relationship with us?
- What if our customers exhibited the ideal behavior profile (for instance, bought all product/service lines, used them exclusively, and paid full price)?
- How long (on average) do customers remain with our organization?
- What if our customers remained customers for life...what would be the cause?

Along with self awareness and interpersonal insight, we see the process of defining success requirements as a key component of any large-scale transformational change. The fourth transformation cornerstone is change mechanisms.

Change Mechanisms

The change mechanism answers the question; "By what method will organizational change be accomplished?" We believe change mechanisms must be strategic, comprehensive, and integrate change at all organizational levels (business process, group/team, and individual).

For the better part of thirty years, North American businesses and industries have faced the challenge of improving performance in order to continue to exist in the world marketplace. Efforts to create breakthroughs in key results areas and to face new competition have evolved from small, singularly focused projects to large-scale, multi-front improvement programs spanning many years. When working to improve organizations, particularly large ones, change masters are often overwhelmed by the magnitude of the effort.

Many change masters lack knowledge and skills associated with such large-scale change initiatives. The basic skills required for this work include:

- strategic planning (mission, vision, values, strategies, tactics);
- learning systems;
- visible measurement scorecards;

- infrastructures for change;
- culture change approaches;
- motivation systems; and
- process improvement techniques.

Not only is expertise in these areas required, but their integration is essential.

A Strong Foundation

As you have seen, self awareness, interpersonal insight, requirements for success, and change mechanisms support each other and are interrelated. These four transformation cornerstones can provide a strong foundation to an integrated, comprehensive and strategic approach to organizational change. The key is to balance them so that none is forgotten and none gets too far in front of the others.

SUMMARY POINTS

- Spirituality is the connection of people with each other and to their source.

- Awakening the spirit is a crucial element for successful individual, group, and organizational transformation.

- Miracles occur when individuals start to transform and balance all aspects of life, including personal growth, family, work, and community.

- Seven elements are of great value in facilitating spiritual awakening in the workplace:
    - Leadership
    - Evolution
    - Expression
    - Play
    - Beauty
    - Choice
    - Love

- Four cornerstones create a foundation for organizational transformation:
    - Self Awareness
    - Interpersonal Insight
    - Requirements for Success
    - Change Mechanism

QUESTIONS and REFLECTIONS

How do I accept and display my natural abilities to lead?

How am I playing a conscious role in my evolution?

Where am I most and least evolved as a creative spirit?

How do I express myself at home and at work?

What fears do I refuse to release?

How often do I play? Why do I not play more often?

Which dimensions of my life are not fun?

What parts of myself do I consider to be beautiful/not beautiful?

Is it difficult for me to see beauty in everyone I meet?

How often do I exercise the principle that "attitude is a choice?"

How do I express love at work?

What is my self awareness process?

In what ways are my interpersonal insight skills lacking?

What are the requirements for success for my organization?

Chapter 2

EXPAND YOUR POTENTIAL

"Ultimately, man should not ask what the meaning of his life is, but rather he must recognize that it is he who is asked ... each man is questioned by life; and he can answer to life by answering for his own life; to life he can only respond by being responsible."

- Victor Frankl

Y ou have unlimited potential. In this chapter, we introduce ways to expand your potential through self awareness and moving towards personal mastery. Prepare to learn about creating results that you never thought possible.

Specifically, we offer tools and methods that support emergence of your personal and spiritual energy. Then in Chapter 3, we reveal key components to help direct your spiritual energy to lead organizational transformation. Finally, in Chapters 4 and 5, we describe how you can create necessary and meaningful connections among coworkers and engage them in transforming the organization.

Personal mastery is a path on which you explore and practice making your realized results match your desires and pronouncements. If you choose this path, you will want to engage in a self awareness process. With self awareness, you pursue an inner journey to face the internal barriers inhibiting your growth and development. Among these barriers are your fears, unproductive views of reality, self-judgment, self-doubt and questions of self-worth. This is where your demons lie, but it is also where insight, joy, beauty and love prevail.

Love and Fear

Neale Donald Walsh (1996) shared in his book, *Conversations with God,* that as life spirits we choose between two opposite ends of a spectrum. On one end is love and on the other end is fear. Both play a part in our ability to create.

It takes courage and a love of creating to trust our creative energy. It also requires a renouncement of the fear of creation. Whenever fear is a stumbling block, we can acknowledge the fear and learn from it. We can also choose to love being in connection with an even more powerful source.

We all have strong inner critics, reminding us of our failures, telling us to stop before we embarrass ourselves, and imploring us not to dig deeper because it is too difficult. Going deeper requires risk taking. Once you have taken the risk, you must be willing to give birth to what emerges, regardless of its form.

Mom and I were in the waiting area at the hospital emergency room. My father had been taken there an hour earlier with severe chest pains. The door opened and a doctor said, "I'm so sorry, he's gone." My mom burst out crying, and I got very calm. I went to the phone and called my aunts. They said, "We're on our way." I asked the doctor if I could go back and see my father. Don't remember much about walking into the room, just that the man lying on the table was so swollen and bruised I didn't recognize him at first. I went over and held my dad's hand, rubbed a little patch of his arm that wasn't covered over with tubes or tape. I said some things like, "Thank you for all you've taught me." "Thank you for being my father." "I'm proud of you." "I love you." The words just came out. I don't recall consciously directing them, but when I spoke I knew they were true. Then my dad's body jerked. He opened his eyes a little, looked at me and nodded. The doctor yelled and the room filled up with white coats. Somebody pulled me back out to the waiting area. The next thing I remember is my aunts showing up and me trying to explain what had happened. That was five years ago. My dad is going strong today. And I'm going strong too, because I know for a fact what's the most powerful force in the universe — it's love.

Miracles and You

Work miracles begin when you release firm assertions concerning what it takes to transform or change. This means setting aside others' opinions and all social comparisons. Miracles then have the opportunity to develop as you release excuses, expectations, and filters.

Success is strengthened when you choose to take a spiritual journey through the unknown. On this journey you confront the past, challenge your fears, and push the personal envelope. Expanding your potential is difficult because you must visit unfamiliar places to face your inner critics. You must learn to connect with your source and develop the courage to seek your inner truth.

You can face your demons and direct your special insights into meaningful results. In this process, you can find the inner core that holds honesty, delusion, beauty, and pain. Keep your environment in mind, because self awareness flourishes in an atmosphere where both the soul and the creation process are accepted and ultimately honored.

Often, the energy bound up in guilt, pain, denial or repression can be positively transformed and unleashed to create phenomenal results. It begins by tapping into the beauty and strength of your inner diamond and into the unlimited energy emitted from your source. You might then move on to guide others to face their own demons.

JOHARI'S SELF-AWARENESS WINDOW

Where do you start? Johari's Window is one model you can use to support your journey to personal mastery. The use of Johari's Window allows your friends, family, and associates to help you evaluate what you do not know about yourself. There are four panes (or quadrants) in this window as seen in Figure 3.

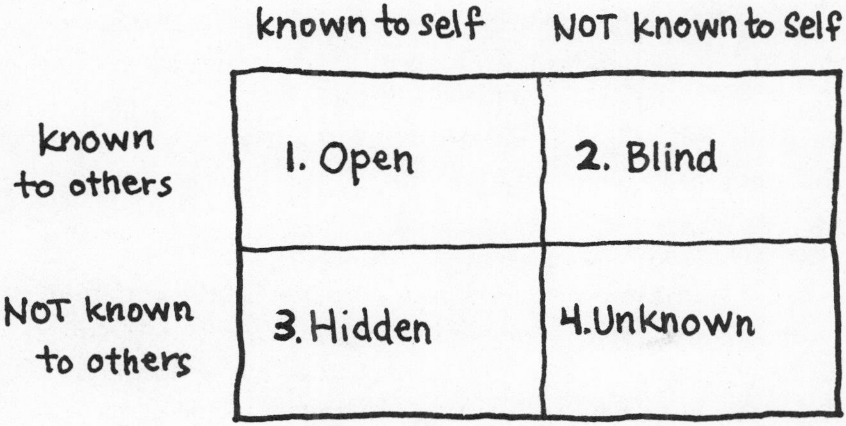

	known to self	NOT known to self
known to others	1. Open	2. Blind
NOT known to others	3. Hidden	4. Unknown

Figure 3: Johari's Window

Quadrant 1: What you know and others know about you.

Quadrant 2: What you do not know but others know about you.

Quadrant 3: What you know but others do not know about you.

Quadrant 4: What you and others do not know about you.

The key opportunity lies in Quadrant 2. In order to know yourself better, it helps if you collect as much information as possible from those around you. This input coupled with introspection can be most enlightening. Quadrant 2 shrinks slowly because your defense mechanisms can blind you in areas that threaten your self-concept.

Many methods are available to help you learn what you do not know about you. These methods include self-assessment tools and value-added feedback from co-workers. The key is in your decision to learn more about yourself and seek the methods that are right for you.

BE, DO, HAVE

On the journey of self awareness, you must get in touch with three basic aspects of life: 1) *being*, 2) *doing*, and 3) *having*. *Being* is aliveness and consciousness. *Doing* is action and directed energy. *Having* is coexisting with things and people around you. Each component supports the other two.

A key to self awareness is to *be* true to yourself, then *do* what gives you joy in order to *have* what you want. Many approach this backwards. They start with *having* or *doing* in order to *be* happy (Gawain, 1991).

For example, take the process of becoming a physician. On one hand, one might approach getting (*having*) a medical degree as the way to practice (*do*) medicine and thus become (*be*) a physician. On the other hand, as a healer (*be*) one might be involved (*do*) in the medical arts field and want to develop skills and benefit from the knowledge of others and therefore, attend medical school. As an outcome of medical school, one would obtain (*have*) a medical degree.

We recommend that you start with concentrating on *being*. From there *do* what gives you joy, and you will *have* in abundance what you desire. Think about it. Many people use the term *Supreme Being* to acknowledge their source. To make our point, we call to attention that we have yet to hear of the terms *Supreme Doing* or *Supreme Having*.

Working with many industries, groups and organizations over the years, we have known people who wanted to bring about change. In many instances, the same people who were enthusiastic at the beginning were not truly prepared to enroll themselves in the experience of self awareness when confronted with the requirements to release excuses, expectations and filters. In these cases, conditioning of the mind was essential. We have discovered that in the end change is about intention.

THE POWER OF INTENTION

So if you are to change, how do you do it? At the individual level, exercising choice, taking risks, and holding a proper attitude are critical to clear intention. Intention means paying attention to your desired outcome with such unbending, laser-like purpose that you absolutely refuse to allow obstacles to dissipate the focused quality of your attention (Chopra, 1994).

The results you create are an absolute function of intention. As a matter of fact, intention underlies all personal and organizational transformation. Change mechanisms are just tools and not the key leverage point. Intention has a 100 percent relationship to whether or not results are achieved.

You achieve the result you intend to create — either consciously or unconsciously. Even when you do not have the right mechanisms, if your intention is clear you will create your desired results. You will find everything you need to achieve your intended outcomes, including the appropriate mechanisms. If you have clear intention to be, do and have, you are positioned to expand your potential and make change happen.

The word "intention" is used here to describe conscious or unconscious desires to deliver meaningful results. Stated boldly, your results become the direct outcome of your intention. Personal outcomes, such as your health, wealth, and relationships, are the demonstrated result of your intentions. You are as fit as you intend to be, make the money you intend to make, and have the quality of relationships you intend to have.

The Issue of Choice

When we explore the reasons or barriers that prevent us from having clear intention, often what is revealed are the choices we make about our barriers. For example, let us consider the issue of money. If you were asked whether you currently make the amount you intend to, what would be your answer? Typically, the answer is, "No." Well, why not rob a bank? The answer is linked to a moral code about stealing or the risk level involved.

Personal behavior choices, such as the way we make money, reflect our values and how they relate to the declared result (money). For example, we could rob banks or hold a legitimate job in order to have money. The process and the goal reflect our values (choosing to obey or disobey laws against robbing banks). So, by choosing not to rob a bank, we have revealed our true intentions, given our choices, to be law abiding citizens.

By discovering our true intention and gaining a higher level of awareness, we can shift our focus from barriers and use creativity to realize our goals. If our true intention (the will) is to be law abiding and then to make considerable money, our creativity will find mechanisms (the way) to accomplish this aim.

Within organizations, much intention work can be done at the individual and small group levels. This work is necessary to build a sense of group community. Just as an athlete works to reach top physical condition, significant mental conditioning is needed to undertake a transformation effort. The challenge is to condition the mind by releasing ways of thinking that do not support positive change and embracing those that do support taking risks to increase effectiveness.

Risk and Increasing Effectiveness

We encourage you to explore your personal paradigms, to experiment and take risks. We invite you to move beyond your comfort zones, and to practice new ways of thinking and acting. We challenge you to engage in emotional or risky behaviors that push your limits.

For example, discuss your current level of trust with some of the people you know. You may find this frightening. In many workplaces, mutual trust is rarely discussed with peers, customers, or suppliers.

Some people find they are not as uncomfortable as they expected and experience benefits from taking such risks. Risks provide opportunities for you to experience new emotions and develop new skills. Risk taking can be a mechanism to increase personal effectiveness.

Risks allow you to get outside your comfort zone and to see the positive consequences of behaving with choice. Proactively being uncomfortable also increases your personal effectiveness by broadening your knowledge base as a result of expanded experiences. Risk taking can also help adjust and expand a narrow and improper attitude.

Attitude Is A Choice

In any situation you can control one thing — your attitude. Attitude comes from past experiences. You develop a comfort zone around your current attitudes toward different people, places, and things. Your attitudes are not inherently good or bad. However, to grow and change you need to be aware of your attitudes and be willing to examine them.

How does this work in an organizational setting? The organization is a collection of people and teams. We all want to create great organizations with outstanding people. We believe people who are risking and growing tend to live fuller, more enjoyable, and more productive lives than those who are not. They are more likely to see that they can choose their attitudes and behaviors.

The key question is, do you control your attitudes or do they control you? To examine your attitudes, you must be willing to experiment and maybe even to be wrong. In many groups, looking good and being right are all that seem to matter. Real change begins with understanding that attitude is a choice. It also involves choosing a mental stance.

At-Effect versus an At-Cause Mental Stance

This leads back to the concepts of at-cause and at-effect, discussed in Chapter 1. At the core of these concepts is the idea of choosing a mental stance from which to operate and live your life. Our experience is that choosing one mental stance creates a different set of results in your life than choosing the other.

At-effect individuals see themselves as victims. They believe things happen to them. They experience events as occurring outside their control. They do not look at or see how events connect with their lives. At-effect individuals produce stories or reasons why things are less than they could be.

By contrast, at-cause individuals create the results they desire in their lives. They see themselves as accountable for making things happen around them. They want to touch the important elements of their lives. Constantly on the outlook for how all people are connected to each other and their source, individuals who are at-cause do not see people and events in isolation. Instead, they perceive them as being interrelated and painting a colorful mosaic. Focused, at-cause individuals consciously create their desired results.

The following sections discuss four areas of understanding we have identified as absolutely essential if you choose an at-cause mental stance on the path of personal mastery: transcending internal barriers; understanding the relationship between intention and results; planning your desired future; and increasing your levels of effectiveness.

I grew up with the naïve perception that I was going to lead a charmed life. But when I left the nest at 18, it didn't take long for me to experience my first taste of failure and disappointment. A long-term relationship ended, I struggled in my college classes, lost a part-time job, the usual "school of hard knocks" stuff. Except it was happening to me. Of course, I didn't want to face my connection to these events... it was easier and more gratifying to find someone or something else to blame. So I started creating victim stories.

My stories were a constant source of comfort and entertainment for me. Certain stories I would actually REHEARSE! I had SCRIPTS! And like grandmothers who pull out photo albums of their grandkids, I could pull out my collection of victim stories at the drop of a hat ... and ...eventually... I became the victim of my victim stories. And who knows what would have happened if some people in my life hadn't stopped enabling me to play victim? Who knows? I suspect my transformation story would have stopped at Chapter 1.

Here is my life story as I once told it, back when I chose to be a victim:

- *I had a difficult birth and some remnants of that experience still plague my psyche.*

- *I am an only child and never learned to socialize properly.*

- *I'm from the rural South, and people automatically associate that with ignorance and poverty.*

- *I am a Scorpio...so don't blame me for my fits of temper.*

- *My father was emotionally distant; therefore I <u>fill in the blank</u>. (NOTE: I got A LOT of mileage out of this one.)*

- *I received an inferior high school education and wasn't prepared for college.*

- *I was out sick the day they covered this.*

- *He made me so upset that I <u>fill in the blank</u> (typically involved food, alcohol, revenge, going home to mother, or some combination of all four.)*

- *My job? You want to know about my JOB? Well, basically I keep this entire operation running, but do I get even as much as a thank you? I WOULD just QUIT, but I've only got two years until I'm vested.*

The End.

TRANSCENDING INTERNAL BARRIERS

Most barriers to achieving your goals lie within you. Carl Jung, the noted psychologist, observed that opportunity for individual growth is found by bringing the unconscious self into awareness. Consider the iceberg as a model for thinking about your self awareness.

An iceberg is only about 10 percent visible above the water, with the other 90 percent being submerged. Likewise, your current level of self-knowledge compared to your potential level of self awareness is small. Like the iceberg, much of your self awareness is submerged in an unconscious state. Consequently, most of your baggage, paradigms, intention, history, culture, programming, reaction, and instinct are unknown to you.

Most internal struggles arise because you lack awareness of how the unconscious mind places limitations on you. To achieve your goals, you need to be aware of the internal barriers and fear-based beliefs that stop your achievement. You can surface these hidden intentions through directed and constructive introspection and by actively processing feedback from others. Remember Johari's Window? Using Quadrant 2 to find out what others know about you that you do not know can be extremely enlightening.

By obtaining the observations of others, the process becomes more efficient. Surfacing what you subconsciously know and bringing your intentions into consciousness is a lifetime endeavor. When you learn to view yourself by standing back and seeing yourself in action, tremendous headway can be made.

Self-observation is a learned skill. By focused practice and suspended judgment, a new perspective is possible. It can be equated to running your mental video recorder of the world, but with you in the picture. Normally you tape what your eyes see. Usually, that means that you are not in the picture, unless you are looking in a mirror.

Part of achieving personal mastery is clarity of intention. When you have clear intention to be, do, or have something, it becomes manifest. To gain clear intention, you must get in touch with your inner spirit. This inner self is a fountain of insight, joy, and beauty. There are many ways to connect with this inner energy such as prayer, meditation, and visualization.

Establishing a conscious connection to your source is important. This connection brings guidance from a deeper wisdom, which makes choices and creation more pure, powerful, and purposeful. Seeking connection to the source drives discovery of self and clear intention. You then make choices that reveal your intention.

When you can see the power of creating your life's story, you can write your own scripts. You can transcend fear. You then find the means to achieve your stated vision. Your demonstrated intention is found in what you accomplish. This leads to greater awareness from which emerges the opportunity to further influence your future with more choices.

YOUR PERSONAL BLUEPRINT

What is the opportunity? The opportunity is to discover your life's purpose and to create, instead of simply react, to your current environment. Discovering your purpose in life is easier said than done. But without a purpose, wandering aimlessly becomes the course of choice. Once your personal purpose becomes focused, strategic direction and tangible goals can be formed.

The process of setting direction and goals facilitates the creation of what you want in life. You can then sharpen your life's direction and change your goals as often as needed. Goals give you a clear focal point on which to direct your natural creativity. In the context of personal mastery, goals serve as a path toward inspiration and creation.

Overcoming Resistance

We have discovered that the process of goal formation can elicit emotional resistance in some people. This resistance takes different forms, such as depression, hopelessness, confusion, denial, anger, and fear. If this happens, we recommend that you experience and process these responses rather than repress them. If you need professional help to do this, get it.

We acknowledge that addressing your feelings and fears can be painful. However, you benefit through overcoming your own subconscious resistance. This very resistance is a roadblock to establishing your path. It all comes back to raising your level of consciousness.

Creating a personal blueprint gives you a deeper understanding of your self, your goals, and your fears. Immersing your self in the goal-setting process forces you to visualize where you want to be and how to get there.

It also heightens your awareness of how far you currently are from your desired state. The distance of this gap can be discouraging and even painful. On the other hand, you can choose to enjoy the personal planning process.

Individual Development Document

In our public seminars, we open with the question, "Why are you here?" You can imagine the many different responses offered. Replies cover a wide spectrum from "Seeking specific technical knowledge," to "I was told to attend by my boss."

Often in the mix are some completely blank faces as well. We rarely have people answer the question, "Why are you here?" with clarity.

It is easy to jump into an activity, such as a public seminar, without understanding its connection to a higher purpose. This is especially true if you are not personally and spiritually aware and if you have not chosen an at-cause mental stance. Beneath the question, "Why are you here?" are questions such as, "What is the purpose of your life?" and "Why are you here in this life on this planet at this point in time?"

Without some understanding of your life's purpose, it is hard to discover if you find true meaning in attending a seminar, or more importantly, in your daily work, activities and relationships. One method that has been helpful to us, is the Individual Development Document (IDD) process. Using the IDD, you can get in touch with your higher self and use that wisdom to achieve meaningful and tangible goals.

This process requires total self-honesty. No one ever needs to see your IDD. Your IDD is a tailored road map to personal mastery. It is used to derive consciousness and clarity of your intentions. In the next section, we describe the process of developing a personal IDD.

The IDD Process

In the IDD process, you complete five sets of questions designed to evoke focused introspection and self awareness. It is crucial that you write your responses to the IDD. Writing helps articulate and distill your inner thoughts more clearly. Figure 4 illustrates the IDD.

1. Conceptual Image of Yourself, both Personal and Professional

- Who are you?
  - What do you do?
  - Who do you do it with?
  - What value do you add to your customers? To your organization? To the world?
  - How do you introduce yourself? Who do you say you are to others?
- What are your personal strengths? Why? What are your technical and professional competencies?
- What are your weaknesses? Why?
- What do you have passion for? What gives you joy?
- Who do you learn from? What are you learning from them? To whom are you a mentor? What are they learning from you?
- How well do you manage the agreements you make with others and yourself? How do you manage trust with others? How trustworthy are you?
- What results are you producing? Why? How do you achieve results? What is your approach when results are not forthcoming?

2. Purpose, Personal and Professional Vision

- What is your life's purpose? Why are you here?
- If your life were on tape, and you fast forwarded the tape so that you were at the end looking back, what would you see? How would you feel?
- What in your past would you change?

3. Goals and Objectives (2-5 years), both Personal and Professional

- What are your goals and objectives?
- What areas in your life do these goals and objectives encompass? What areas are not addressed?
- How would you know if these goals and objectives were accomplished?

4. Near Term Actions (3 - 6 months)

- What actions will you take to improve yourself personally and professionally? What results do you expect to create in the next 3-6 months?
  - To fulfill your life's purpose?
  - To move toward your vision?
  - To move toward your goals and objectives?
- What will you experiment with? What risks will you take?
- What will you read?
  - Do?
  - Study?
  - Experience?
- What feedback will you seek?
- What relationships will you create, mend or improve?
- How will you build agreements and trust?

5. In Relationship to the Organization

- How do you see yourself connected to your organization's transformation effort now?
- In 2 years?
- In 5 years?

Figure 4: Individual Development Document

The IDD considers the whole person by encompassing both personal and professional dimensions. IDDs do not have to be shared with others. A key benefit of the IDD is that it provides a means by which you can articulate your vision and goals. You can then compare the vision and goals of the organization to your own in order to check for alignment. The IDD is best kept simple and flexible allowing changes to be made when needed.

The IDD is for the individual. It is not an evaluation tool. Instead, it is an improvement tool. It is intended to facilitate and spark critical introspection. It is intended to assist with increasing consciousness and clarity. The IDD is a dynamic and living document, intended to be updated from Version 1.0 to Version 2.0, and so on.

The Life Plan

Your Individual Development Document leads toward your Life Plan. The Life Plan is a written document in which you express your plan for the future in critical life areas. The Life Plan takes the information provided in the IDD and translates it into a long-term vision and nearer-term goals for specific areas of life, such as spiritual, family, physical, intellectual, professional and financial. It also describes events that were milestones of your past. These events give historical perspective to the you that exists today. Figures 5a and 5b outline the additional information that, together with the IDD form the draft of a Life Plan. A complete Life Plan form can be found in Appendix A. The format in the appendix is slightly different, allowing variation in writing space to capture your full thoughts. Of course, your personal life plan may have different areas of focus according to your personal interests, vision and goals.

SIGNIFICANT LIFE EVENTS

A significant life event is a specific happening...a critical incident...a key episode in your past, set in a particular time and place. It is a specific moment in your life that stands out to you for some reason. Describe several of the most critical incidents in your life to date. What was the impact of these events on the course of your life and who you are as a person?

MY...	SIGNIFICANT LIFE EVENTS	THEIR IMPACT ON ME
SPIRIT		
MIND		
BODY		
FAMILY		
FINANCES		
WORK		
COMMUNITY		

Figure 5a: Life Plan Worksheet 1

MAKING THE VISION A REALITY

In order to build creative tension, it is important to define your intended Point of Arrival (desired future state), your Point of Departure (current state), and what it will take to Close the Gap (actions required to reach your Point of Arrival). You can use this template as a worksheet to draft your Point of Arrival, Point of Departure, and path to Close the Gap.

MY...	POINT OF DEPARTURE Current State	PATH TO CLOSE THE GAP Actions Required to Reach my Point of Arrival	INTENDED POINT OF ARRIVAL Short Term Goals (12-18 months) Long Term Vision		
SPIRIT	Where am I now in my spiritual development?		Goals I will achieve toward creating my spiritual being	Be:	Do:	Have:
MIND	Where am I now in my intellectual growth?		Goals I will achieve in developing my mind	Be:	Do:	Have:
BODY	What condition is my physical body in?		Physical fitness goals	Be:	Do:	Have:
FAMILY	Current condition of my family?		Goals I will achieve in building my family	Be:	Do:	Have:
FINANCES	What is my current financial status? How do I view $$?		Financial goals and my relationship to wealth	Be:	Do:	Have:
WORK	Where am I in regards to my chosen vocation?		Vocational goals, what my work will look like	Be:	Do:	Have:
COMMUNITY	What is my community life like?		Goals in building the community I desire	Be:	Do:	Have:

Figure 5b: Life Plan Worksheet 2

61

INTENTION \ MECHANISM \ RESULTS

Once you are aware of personal barriers and have a firm direction, you can employ growth mechanisms and tools to move from your Point of Departure to your desired Point of Arrival. Mechanisms are just tools or approaches to achieve personal goals, which then support your purpose and intention.

As an example, one's purpose might be to "equip youth for living an enriched life." A goal might be, "I want to work full time with pre-school children for a year so I can help build their self awareness." A mechanism that might facilitate this goal is a stand-alone day care center. However, when executing this mechanism for change, it might become obvious that establishing a day care center in the existing community involves more resources than anticipated.

With a clear view of the goal and its relationship to one's life purpose, one could then look at different mechanisms to achieve the goal of working with children for a year to build their self awareness. One could work in a day care center initially while building resources, establish a smaller in-home center, or be where children are present such as a hospital or social welfare environment. A clear understanding of one's goal coupled with the creative mind can drive discovery of the mechanisms needed to accomplish the desired result. While devoting energy to mechanisms can move one forward, only 100 percent intention to achieve a goal ensures that results are created.

Figure 6 speaks to two ways of viewing the results we create. We believe that your results are driven by your intention. Others might argue that when results fall short, there must have been some external happening, a mechanism failure that prevented the result from matching stated desires. Excuses or stories are formed to rationalize this performance.

If a 70 percent result is produced, then a corresponding 30 percent story would be needed to explain why 100 percent performance was not the result. If you are 10 minutes late for a meeting, a 10-minute excuse is needed. Then the excuse centers on the mechanisms that prevented you attending the meeting (e.g., traffic, demanding situation, alarm clock).

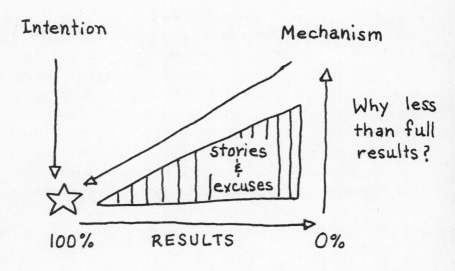

Figure 6: Intention / Mechanism / Results

Your true intention is indicated by your demonstrated results. Said another way, by reviewing your results in life, your past intentions are made evident. The life you have created is the life you intended to create, consciously or unconsciously. For some, this is difficult to accept. The tendency is to point to external barriers that have kept life from turning out as desired.

But imagine receiving a call at work where you learn that your close family member is seriously ill and desperately needs you in attendance. Would you consider barriers to leaving work in the same light as say, leaving early to perform overdue household chores? No, you would transcend barriers and find a way to get to your ailing loved one because of clear intention.

On the other hand, you might point to breakdowns in mechanisms (employment responsibilities) in order to explain why your household chores did not get done. In fact, the mechanisms did not prevent your chores from being done. It was an intentional choice not to do the household chores, and it was an intentional choice to meet your employment responsibilities. The key is being honest with yourself and acknowledging your intention as opposed to creating excuses that blame other people, events or things. Getting clear on your intention can increase your personal effectiveness.

LEVELS OF EFFECTIVENESS

A father was teaching his daughter, Jessica, to ride a bicycle. Finally came the day when she was riding the bike with some expertise. She was on the road and doing okay.

Eventually, the father told her to ride down to the house. The area was a little steep, but not unsafe, and had one oak tree in front of the house. As Jessica started down the hill, the father shouted, "Don't run into the oak tree!"

Immediately, as her father's shout called her to focus, Jessica started heading toward the oak tree. The father yelled again, "Watch out for the tree, Jessica!" As you can imagine, she hit it straight on.

Afterwards, Jessica believed that all oak trees and hills were dangerous. Every time she saw an oak tree, her brain played a tape that oak trees were dangerous. At that point, it was easy for her to stay in her comfort zone by avoiding trees and hills.

This comfort zone, however, came to limit her perspective, potential, and possibilities. What eventually shook Jessica out of her comfort zone? She wanted to explore her hilly and tree-filled neighborhood on her bicycle.

Where she wanted to go (her point of arrival) was more compelling than staying where she was (her point of departure). Thus, she intended to create a different result (close the gap).

Our experience shows that there is more power in such a vision than in a burning platform. What is a burning platform? A burning platform equates to the negative consequences we believe are possible if we do not move off of a platform that is being burned away by change. John F. Kennedy used vision, not a burning platform, to inspire and evoke action and inspiration in the United States' exploration of space.

Kennedy did not say "Let me tell you how pitiful we

are. Those Russians are beating us! We will be ruined." Instead he said, "We do this and other things, not because they are easy but because they are hard. And it brings out the best in us as a people and a nation."

And now back to Jessica. At first she did not understand how hills and trees related to bicycle riding. Then she crashed, and was thrown into a state of mystery about hills, trees and such. So she created a comfort zone (tape or paradigm) that hills and trees are dangerous. Encouraged by her father to try the hill again, she found it very easy to rationalize her own tapes, "Of course hills are dangerous. Just look at what happened to me the last time I rode on one."

However, because Jessica had a vision of riding around her hilly neighborhood with her friends, she chose to break out of her comfort zone and take a risk. She continued to experiment and observe herself and eventually had an insight, which led to breakthroughs in her cycling performance. With continued practice and feedback, she eventually mastered her hilly, tree-filled neighborhood. We call this Levels of Effectiveness, which is illustrated in Figure 7.

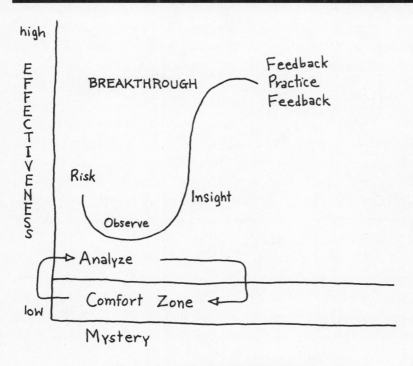

Figure 7: Levels of Effectiveness

Levels of Effectiveness illustrate that you create tapes or a comfort zone when in mystery. Staying in your comfort zone is easy and requires taking a risk in order to break free of it. You must create clear intention in order to take the risk. Once the risk is taken, if you make careful observations, you can gain insight and experience breakthroughs.

Following repeated practice and feedback, you have the opportunity to increase your effectiveness. Then, as you might have guessed, the process starts all over again if you choose to

67

move to a higher level of effectiveness. This framework is applicable in all areas of your life and is especially powerful if you set up the right conditions for your success.

CREATE THE RIGHT CONDITIONS

As you begin the self awareness process, we recommend you ensure the following conditions of success are present. First, assume an at-cause mental stance, taking responsibility for you rather than controlling, analyzing or blaming other people, events, and things. Second, approach the personal mastery process voluntarily. Third, realize that you are part of the creation of your life's results.

Additional success factors include self-honesty, self-disclosure and social support. Prepare to open up to rigorous self-examination and genuine sharing. Develop friendships and mentoring relationships with those on a similar path. Through these relationships, self awareness will become interwoven with the fabric of your day-to-day life.

Last but not least, optimism is essential. In order to achieve it, find safe environments in which expressions of non-materialistic, altruistic, and spiritual values are celebrated. Such environments will be supportive of your pursuits, struggles and creations.

THE CRITICAL STEPS TO SELF AWARENESS

In order to put the learnings in this chapter into practice, we find that seven steps are critical including:

1. Intend to "Be"

Make a conscious commitment to follow your truth and to do whatever it takes to learn, grow, heal, gain awareness and "be." You may want to make this commitment privately or with a partner, family member, friends, or team. You may seek assistance of a facilitator in any of these forums. If you wish, you can make a statement of intention and create a ritual to formalize the event by writing it in a journal, meditating in a special place, or saying it in a natural setting.

2. Listen to Your Inner Spirit

Develop a relationship with your own inner spirit by practicing the art of listening to and following your intuition. Discover the connection of your inner spirit with your greater source and tap into that power.

3. Learn Methods and Acquire Skills

Investigate new tools and resources including books, tapes, lectures, and mentors. It is also okay to release all such mechanisms and just "be" when necessary.

4. Allow Time for Restoration of the Diamond

Devote time to restoring the brilliance of your diamond. The personal mastery process is the rediscovery of the clarity and power of our inner diamond or spirit. We all are wounded to some degree. Restoration of the diamond may take more energy for some than for others. Regardless of the tools and techniques we have chosen, relearning to love the self is no small task.

5. Discover Support

Find the support needed for your journey. You may feel guilty or ashamed to ask for help. No one wants to be vulnerable. But the path of personal mastery is far too long and complex to manage alone. Once you look for help, you will find many people wanting to honor your journey with assistance. A wealth of support is available for the asking. There is one caution, however. You must be able to discern the people who provide truth and energy in their approach from those driven by fear, who wish to drain your energy with criticism and sabotage.

6. Relax, Release and Create

Express your creative energy. This may be difficult if you have a lot of mental clutter. Often internal chaos has built up over the years as a result of criticism (from others and from you). Thus, you set unreasonable standards for yourself, which leads to failure and in turn leads to an unwillingness to take risks with creativity. Relaxation is key to releasing your internal chaos and clutter. So relax, release and create!

7. Teach Others

Pass on to others what you learn from this process. Full integration of knowledge is not complete until you pass it on to others — that is true mastery. This does not have to be a painful process, but should be natural and flow from within. As you become more self-aware, you will find new ways to influence the consciousness of others.

SUMMARY POINTS

♦ Self awareness requires taking an inner journey to face the internal barriers inhibiting your growth and mastery.

♦ Johari's Window helps you discover what you do not know about yourself.

♦ On the journey of self awareness, you must get in touch with three basic aspects of life: 1) *being*, 2) *doing*, and 3) *having*.

♦ Intention has a 100 percent relationship to whether or not results are achieved.

♦ Risks allow you to get outside your comfort zone and to see the positive consequences of behaving with choice.

♦ At-cause individuals create the results they desire in their lives; at-effect individuals see themselves as victims.

♦ The process of setting direction and goals facilitates the creation of what you want in life.

♦ A Life Plan includes a long-term vision and nearer-term goals for specific areas of life, such as spiritual, family, physical, intellectual, professional and financial.

QUESTIONS and REFLECTIONS

What is my purpose in life?

What will I "Be" in 10 years? "Do" in 10 years?
"Have" in 10 years?

What tools do I need in order to meet my goals?

What help do I need in acquiring these tools?

How often do I blame others for things that go wrong?

Am I willing to "look in the mirror" regularly? If not, why ?

What are my steps to self awareness?

Where do the opportunities lie in my organization to work miracles?

In which areas of my life do I have clear intention? Where am I
not clear?

What is the difference in the results I create when I have clear
intention versus when I do not?

Where am I blocking my creative energy?

What are the barriers I fear most? Why?

Chapter 3

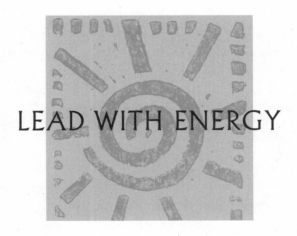

LEAD WITH ENERGY

"The job of the leader/servant is to help build intelligence, judgment and character. It may require significant breaks with traditional ways of seeing and doing."

- Stephen R. Covey

With clear intention and vision, you can lead your organization's transformation. In Chapter 1, we discussed the importance of awakening and nurturing spirituality in the workplace. In Chapter 2, we introduced self awareness as a transformation cornerstone. Now, we build upon Chapters 1 and 2, showing you how to create vision alignment at all levels of your organization.

The process of aligning individual and organizational visions is difficult. Alignment begins with understanding your larger purpose, and it requires your conscious involvement in both individual and organizational strategic planning. Let us explore how vision can fuel the fires of change.

Importance of Organizational Vision

The importance of the organizational vision is well understood by most business leaders. As the saying goes, "When you do not know where you are going, any road will take you there." Without a compelling desired future state, the corporate journey becomes little more than a random walk.

There are many testimonials to the power of vision from Olympic success Carl Lewis to pop-icon Madonna. Having a solid and reachable goal is a required ingredient for any achievement. Unfortunately, leaders tend to choose inadequate approaches to produce a sound collective vision.

From the Mountain Top

In the most common scenario, a select group descends from the mountain top (the annual strategic planning retreat) and proudly displays the result of its effort — the corporate vision statement. A strategic planning retreat may sound fun and exciting to those not yet blessed with the experience. However, if you have ever endured such a meeting you are likely to tell a different story.

Visioning can be difficult and joyless work when the spirit of creation and discovery is destroyed by a mechanistic, "let's get it down on paper and get on with it" mind set. One might then say, "Since so much effort has been expended in the visioning process, the result must be right and good." So, when the hard work is done, it must be time to communicate it to the organization and encourage others to follow.

In this scenario, the next step is to hold alignment sessions throughout the organization advocating the new vision. Information-sharing sessions like these are typically held in a trickle-down fashion (from divisions to branches to work groups and so on), with a mix of flashy, high tech presentations, personal addresses by upper management, and sometimes a comprehensive question and answer period.

Senior management often believes sharing (or imposing) the organizational vision will breathe life into the message. However, the message becomes lost in the delivery. Employees pretend to be interested, even enthusiastic, about the new direction. But all the while, they are waiting for the "new" energy, vision, and direction to erode. Employees adopt the attitude that "all things come to pass." They march in place until the current effort loses its power and a new direction begins to form on the horizon. Open skepticism ("we've done this before and it doesn't work") is eventually replaced by a smile, no follow through, or by visible resistance.

A Twist On History

We have taken liberty to rewrite history to illustrate the folly of traditional organizational visioning efforts. In the first example, imagine a conversation between religious reformer Martin Luther and another German as Luther is nailing his ninety-nine theses to the door of the church.

German: "Say, Martin, what are you doing there?"
Martin Luther: "I am implementing and deploying a change process to establish the Protestant faith."
German: "Well, how long do you expect it will take to make this change happen?"
Martin Luther: "Oh, maybe a few weeks ... however long it takes a critical mass to read this document and buy into my vision."

In the second example, imagine a brief encounter between a member of the United States Continental Congress and a colonial citizen when the former wrote the Bill of Rights.

Citizen: "Mr. Delegate, what have you got there?"
Delegate: "It's a document which limits the power of the crown and guarantees certain inalienable rights and liberties to the people."
Citizen: "Outstanding! And how do you intend to make this change a reality?"
Delegate: "My good man, it's quite simple. We plan to send a few copies to the colonies and one to the King. We will attach an inspiring note, which calls upon everyone to walk the talk. This should be sufficient to create ownership for the new vision."

Silly? Yes. Yet, in today's organizations, some leaders believe that voicing the vision once and posting it will accomplish the job.

THE PROBLEM WITH FORCING COMPLIANCE

Many leaders do not assess the impact of their alignment approach on the workforce. Alignment sessions sometimes have the appearance of a religious cult retreat. Participants understand that they must comply, or the personal consequences will be enormous. The message is clear: Get your arrow facing in the right direction, or psychological and/or physical pain will follow.

Figure 8 illustrates this traditional view of alignment. The outcome of an alignment session based on this model is the conscious or the unconscious bending of personal "arrows" into compliance with the organizational vision. In some cases, it can result in the momentary formation of a personal vision where none existed before.

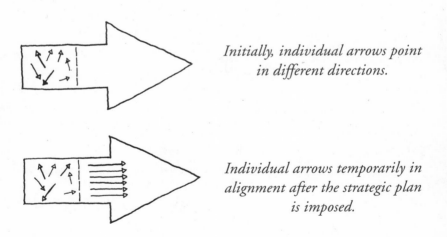

Initially, individual arrows point in different directions.

Individual arrows temporarily in alignment after the strategic plan is imposed.

Figure 8: Traditional Alignment Approach

Those in charge deliver a compelling presentation that the new direction is right for the organization and beneficial to employees. The employee, being reasonable, sees the wisdom in the new direction for the organization. The benefits for the employee usually involve job security, pay adjustments, or other external benefits.

So, the personal sale is made. But this conversion to the organization's vision is often fleeting. After a few days, what made so much sense coming from the vision salesperson does not seem to be what the individual desires. There's a gap — it could be small or large. A strong connection between the individuals' aspirations and those of the organization is missing.

The unanswered questions of spiritual awareness and alignment cause doubt where there was once engagement. Then, the arrows straighten out and individuals return to their previous orientation. True commitment to the organization's plan is again lacking. Those in positions of power are bewildered because employees reverted to status quo behavior.

Those responsible for leading may even cry for additional, and more frequent, alignment sessions. They believe if they can find the right approach for deploying the vision, the right outcome (total organizational alignment) will follow. What people in the organization actually see is wasted time and energy. Scott Adams illustrates this frequently in his *Dilbert* comic strip.

Aligning individual and organizational visions is a difficult process. It requires that individuals have clear direction. All too often employees are largely unaware of what they want for themselves in an organizational setting. They may be well versed in what they do not want in the organization, but this often falls short of defining what they do want.

Effective alignment also requires the organization to have a clear and well-articulated direction. Individuals must have a meaningful context within which to assess the connection between their personal visions and that of the organization. Many authors have summarized this in one word: leadership.

Not long ago, I led an off-site for a newly established department in a large organization. The three day off-site was devoted to, as the top manager put it, "creating a vision that comes alive within every single person in this department." A small group of department employees had met before the off-site to develop a working draft of the vision, which was posted on flipchart paper in very large letters at one end of the meeting room.

That first morning, I asked all thirty participants to stand up and walk to the end of the room opposite the draft vision. I got them all positioned in line, as if they were getting ready to start a race. Then I said, "On the count of three, begin walking toward the posted vision statement, stopping whenever you are at the point that represents your current level of connection to what's written."

As you might imagine, people ended up all over the place. Some participants didn't move forward at all. Others stopped at the mid-way point. And of course, the group who had written the draft marched, as one, all the way up to the flipchart paper.

I said, "Well, it looks like we've got our work cut out for us these next three days."

And work we did.

At the end of the off-site, with my fingers crossed, I asked them to do a final check. Same exercise as the first day, with the newly written vision statement posted. Only this time on the count of three everyone, EVERYONE, ran forward, all the way to the flipchart paper, hugged it, hugged each other, applauded, high-fived, laughed, celebrated.

Like all births, to witness a vision coming alive, it was a blessed event.

HONEST AND AUTHENTIC LEADERSHIP

Leadership is the spiritual energy of an individual or a group of individuals to guide others and accomplish amazing things. We realize this spiritual energy cannot be programmed. It must come from the individual's understanding of a larger purpose for self.

To define one's arrow (personal vision) requires the work of the individual, facilitated through a self awareness process like the one we described in Chapter 2, and it must be supported by the organizational community. Developing a critical mass of people with clarity of purpose and directing that energy productively in the workplace is a necessary step to create a vision community.

When individual energy lines become defined, you can assess what the organization has the energy to accomplish. Figure 9 shows this situation. Individuals become clear on personal vision and then discover how closely it is aligned with the organization's vision. This clarity of direction produces more energy for the organization than a manipulative autocrat could ever generate.

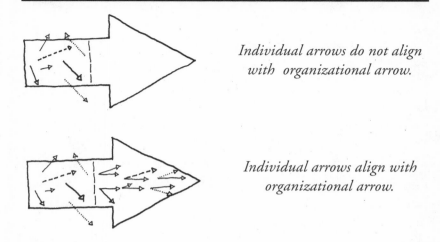

Individual arrows do not align with organizational arrow.

Individual arrows align with organizational arrow.

Figure 9: Vision Community Alignment Approach

MATCHING ENERGIES

By matching individual energies with the organization's requirements, you can assess the probability of reaching defined objectives. It helps to work a simple energy equation. If enough energy is present compared to the energy required, the job can be done. Conversely, if enough energy is not present to accomplish the stated objectives, more energy must be identified, or the job will not get done.

In the case of opposing energy lines, no part of the individual's energy is aligned with the organization. Often the individual will elect to leave the organization due to the obvious mismatch. If not, the organization may choose to end the relationship.

Addressing the Whole Person

After several years of extensive recruiting, key decision makers of a large organization elected to downsize. A meeting with the company hierarchy convinced the plant manager, Jeff, that decreasing total headcount while increasing the employee-to-manager ratio was an achievable goal.

Jeff was energized following the session. He understood the rationale behind the decision. The proposed targets were feasible and, from a corporate strategy standpoint, the choice of making labor adjustments was wise.

Top management identified the lowest performing managers to lay off. Coupled with across-the-board reductions in production employees, this formula would achieve the downsizing targets. Generous packages were provided to all. It was going to be an equitable and benign downsizing.

Jeff's message to the plant management team was short and to the point. He made it clear he cared little for discussion. Members of the team chose not to share their true feelings about the goal or the approach. From past interactions, team members had learned not to voice any objections to the boss's ideas. Despite severe reservations about the game plan, team members dutifully nodded their approval.

Several members accepted the premise to reduce headcount since the decision seemed to make sense for the organization. Other members understood the reason behind the decision but did not accept how it would be implemented. Although these members had reservations, they were fearful of questioning the plan. In short, all the arrows were pointed in the same direction due to perceived coercion.

Shortly after the alignment meeting, hallway discussions began. Members of the plant management had reservations and were quite emotional about letting people go. The plan's execution was disastrous because it lacked personal alignment.

Downsizing throughout the facility continued. Little effort was made to work on the significant emotional impact of the decision. Managers were expected to align with the decision and execute it. Some temporary alignment occurred. However, people's personal arrows quickly returned to their original positions.

In the one-on-one outplacement sessions, the managers were hesitant and lacked enthusiasm. Distrust emerged. Sabotage of the decision became apparent. Slowdowns across the workforce became rampant. Employee relations issues appeared everywhere.

These issues appeared to be unrelated at first, but a pattern emerged. A breakdown in an implied social contract had occurred. The prevailing belief was that if people were loyal to the organization and did their best work, the organization would be loyal to them by giving them job security.

Jeff's failure to address the whole person in the plant management meeting caused major disruptions, misgiving, and distrust among the workforce. If Jeff had sought real alignment, a unified team could have made the labor adjustment work. Furthermore, analysis of over-hiring and subsequent downsizing systems could have helped address the root issues. Given the organizational culture, there was little energy and opportunity to improve a fundamental system flaw.

Creating individual and organizational vision alignment is a process in which individuals are called upon to take risks. They must be intellectually honest and share freely and openly with their colleagues. It also takes a leader or a group of leaders to accomplish and maintain organizational alignment. Finally, you need a process.

VISION ALIGNMENT PROCESS

Based on years of facilitating organizational transformations, we have developed a four-step process to create individual and organizational vision alignment.

In exploring the steps to create alignment, we assume an organizational vision and mission are already in place and a process for strategic planning is being used. Our approach builds upon and focuses existing strategic planning processes. Our crucial and significant addition is the commitment, inspiration, and focus of the whole individual to the attainment of organizational and personal goals. The steps of this process include:

Step 1: Develop collective consciousness of personal visions.

Step 2: Define organizational requirements for success.

Step 3: Declare energy interests.

Step 4: Ensure there is sufficient energy to achieve organizational requirements.

There is a strong correlation between organizational and individual goals. We believe that people will do what needs to be done if their contributions, energies, and inspirations are acknowledged, rewarded, and celebrated. The following describes each step of the process.

Step 1: Develop Collective Consciousness of Personal Visions

Let us assume that personal visions and purpose statements already exist. Sharing these individual visions among the team is critical to developing a collective understanding of where energy lies. In simplest form, you want to understand:

* What brings these people together?
* Where is their common ground?
* Why has each individual chosen to share his or her life's energy with others in the team and this specific organization?
* How conscious are individuals about their own life's purpose and what they want to create?

Understanding and addressing these questions is critical to the organization. A template for recording personal visions called the Individual Development Document was illustrated in Chapter 2. If a collective understanding can be achieved, the team can see greater possibilities to create something of value together. With this knowledge, the team can identify synergistic opportunities, support others' journeys, and avoid misinterpreting actions.

In sharing personal vision statements, a healthy dialogue begins in which common experiences, values, and directions surface. This creates bonding and a desire to focus on the greater good. Gaps and apparent contradictions among people will also surface, providing an opportunity to better understand each other.

In this phase, we suggest active listening, where the listener clarifies, confirms, and summarizes what the sender says. Often, the sender achieves significant insight in hearing someone seek clarification on, or summarize his thoughts. When you share your personal vision statement, the role of the listener is not to help you better present or figure out an improved personal vision. The listener is responsible for developing a deeper understanding of you.

Step 2: Define Organizational Requirements for Success

At this step several important questions arise:

- What is the current purpose and mission of the organization?
- What must the organization be and do in order to prosper in the future?
- What do current and future competitive conditions require the organization to do?
- What does the organization see as success?
- Is survival sufficient or is targeted growth expected?

Addressing these strategic questions helps to start defining organizational success. Defining requirements for success necessitates an external perspective. Scanning the competitive and customer environments ensures that external opportunities and challenges are fully understood and addressed.

The possibility of building a creation community starts at this stage. How leaders choose to conduct the planning effort will either connect people to the strategic creation process or will send the message that only limited personal involvement is required.

The opportunity for leaders to engage the whole individual does not stop with employees but can extend to the organizational stakeholders. Customers, suppliers and other true partners are usually waiting to be asked to join a larger, extended system.

To illustrate this point, the president of a hardware manufacturing firm was wrestling with the recommendation to include key customers and suppliers in the annual strategic planning process. The struggle was not with the suppliers, because he knew he could require their presence. But to invite key customers to the planning process, the least beloved event of the year, was outside everyone's comfort zone.

The political infighting that occurred during these sessions was expected as a result of boredom of the overall process. As the president saw it, valuable customers should not be exposed to strategic planning. Risking major customer relations by letting them see the real organization seemed foolish. However, he decided to give it a shot.

Much to the president's surprise and relief, customers and suppliers developed strong commitments to the firm's direction as a direct result of participating in the planning process. Why? Both the customers and suppliers wanted to be part of something greater than them.

When the energy of participants was exposed — customers and suppliers included — the possibility of creating something greater than the sum of individual ideas captivated them. The customers and suppliers were excited to be part of the proposed creation. The commitments that flowed from suppliers to maintain, and in some cases, reduce prices were unexpected and came from a deeply felt desire to make the collective vision work.

Likewise, key customers committed to be an integral part of increasing unit sales, diversifying products, and ensuring the success of quality initiatives. These commitments came from a spirit beyond self service or manipulation. The thrill of mutual creation that emerged from this strategic planning session proved to be genuine, infectious, and lasting.

Step 3: Declare Energy Interests

Simply put, where do individuals have energy? Having declared what they want to produce and how each wishes to spend their life's energy, what are people passionate about in the workplace? Or expressed another way, where is the match between the spirit and the work?

Decide who is the best person for the work based upon the individual's energy. When this match happens, results exceed expectations. Where alignment of energy and tasks does not exist, work tends to be done listlessly or not done at all. In fact, it is frequently impossible to determine if desired strategies and goals were on target because they were not fully implemented.

First, a draft strategic plan needs to be displayed so that requirements for success are understood. This plan should include honest input from stakeholders. Individuals then review the plan and see which elements inspire them, so that hard commitments follow. From the commitments, an accurate assessment of what will really be done versus what could be done can be determined.

These commitments cannot be forced or extracted from people. The political correctness of signing up to an effort is not part of this process. People are asked to make commitments based on each individual's true desire to create, not for hierarchical recognition—or simply because each is asked to make commitments. It must be an insideout commitment.

Before going further, the word "commitment" must be discussed. Overused and misunderstood, commitment has multiple meanings. Commitments are frequently offered routinely for political gain with little confidence the agreement will be kept.

Judgment about the rightness of making certain commitments must be suspended to understand the nature of the word. It is largely due to the perceived expectations of others that people make commitments which are later broken. You may say you are committed to your family. However, daily actions, attitudes and decisions bear out the accuracy of this assertion. The level of your commitment is evident in deeds — not merely in words. Making commitments builds hope, fulfilling commitments develops trust.

We each have a history of behavior through which others can measure the truthfulness of our pronouncements. The choices you make speak louder than your words. The extent to which you act upon commitment is a true expression of spirit. In this way heartfelt desires and passions are openly displayed. You can test spirit to achieve a certain task before an agreement is made, and can encourage others to hold up a mirror, reflecting back behaviors (feedback) to develop awareness.

In the workplace, when you make conscious commitments, colleagues find they can count on you. Counter-commitments or memos of understanding are no longer required to cover the eventuality of nonperformance. Trust is built in the organization as commitments are made and followed through, and trust is the glue that holds successful organizations together. Seeing a commitment as the natural result of focused energy and intention ensures and strengthens alignment.

There are many methods for declaring energy and commitment. We recommend using creative expression where people commit their names, in writing, to the areas they want to lead or support. Then assertions are made about exactly what individuals are prepared to do. The team, as a whole, tests these assertions based upon their knowledge of the environment and past experiences of the individual. Properly orchestrated, the team can very effectively reveal insincere commitments.

When community exists, the search for unequivocal truth prevails. And when someone declares commitment without spiritual alignment, the team is able to hold up the mirror and help the individual learn more about what is holding him/her back. People become very good at helping each other see the difference between what they should do and what they have a passion to do.

You may have some trouble visualizing this type of interaction given your present situation. Perhaps you do not want to display your true self or do not want to share your personal feelings or thoughts. Initiating a process of open sharing at a deep, personal, and holistic level can seem mysterious and dangerous.

So how do you start? Your personal need must be greater than the risk involved. Personal need is the degree to which you want to create something new or challenging in the workplace.

The above process works and is good for individuals and organizations. We suggest that you try it. It has led to workplace alignment and community. There are other paths leading to the same destination. The real question is whether you have sufficient personal need and urgency to start your journey.

Step 4: Ensure Sufficient Energy to Achieve Organizational Requirements

Is the organization's composite energy sufficient to meet the strategic plan's requirements? In the end, people will do what they have energy to do. Therefore, you need to discover the magnitude and direction of the total organization's energy.

Is there enough energy to assume successful implementation? If there is not sufficient energy, what do you do? Assume the strategic plan is represented by numerous initiatives that require significant time and resources. The declarations of individual energy address a large percentage of the items but several still remain. A key insight: The plan in its entirety was not going to be accomplished anyway, despite promises to the contrary. With honest declarations of energy, the team is in a better position to envision and attain the future reality.

Top leadership may not like it, but the organization has a more accurate assessment of the spirit, energy, commitment, and inspiration to attain the vision. It is now time to ask if the strategic elements lacking energy and commitment need to be accomplished or are they simply pet projects that failed to garner broad-based support or interest. If the last few items are indeed critical, the challenge is to find individuals outside the existing groups who will tackle these projects. The next step is to enroll these individuals.

Accomplishing Results

The outcome of this four-step process is a real commitment to achieve a collective vision that holds passion and is spiritually connected for individuals. Why does this approach of identifying collective vision and applying conscious energy produce different results? When the planning process is designed to address the whole person, a more true and straightforward plan emerges; people can see their connection and contribution.

Using energy as the criterion for owning organizational goals is unlike assigning or choosing ownership based on position, pay grade, or functional expertise. This is a fundamental shift to align personal energy and life's mission to the work of the organization. Work commitments are made based on what individuals have passion to accomplish.

SKILLS AND STRATEGIES

In the four-step process for creating vision and energy alignment, certain leadership skills and strategies are critical for implementation. Most leadership researchers make a clear distinction between being a good manager and being a true leader. While both roles are crucial, managers are people who direct and organize. Good managers are people who do these things well. Leaders, on the other hand, are people who attract others with their thoughts, words and deeds. Leaders share their vision and then teach others what it means to become aligned with it and add energy to it.

The manager administers and the leader innovates. One might say that management is of the mind, while leadership is of the spirit. Someone once said that managers' statements end with a period, and leaders' statements end with a question mark. The following describes the essential skills and attributes you can develop to lead energy alignment within your organization.

Guiding Vision

Every leader has a vision and the magnetism to persuade others to follow. A guiding vision illuminates the journey and reveals the destination. Without a vision there is no coordination.

As Joel Barker states, the common characteristic among those who succeed is a clear vision of their future, not in a mystical sense but in terms of their personal outcome, goal, and direction. Of course, to make others aware of their dreams, leaders must communicate them in action, spirit, words, or passion.

Passionate Leadership

Leaders are full of passion. Their approach to life is so enthusiastic that it is contagious. People rallying around a true leader feel energized. Leaders can be passionate about their beliefs, vision, strategies, followers and undertakings.

Passionless people are often seen as robots, going through life feeling little or nothing, even in the most extraordinary situations. Passionate people, on the other hand, feel both strong positive and negative emotions. Their emotional life is richer because they are more engaged. They really experience their feelings. Passion is the inspiration that can drive you to stretch beyond your comfort zone and ask others to go beyond their self-imposed limitations.

I don't seek to be a role model. Just want to live my life as authentically as I know how. I don't have to stand in the spotlight. Just want a space where I'm free to create. I don't aspire to get to the top. Just want to climb toward new heights of learning and experience forever. No limits.

Here is what I bring to the table: energy, courage, compassion, a mind filled with possibilities, and the determination to move mountains if that's what it takes.
Is that leadership?

Integrity Beyond Proof

A true leader is authentic. He or she has integrity that is contagious. It is both seen and felt. Leaders stick to their values, beliefs and ideas. Their followers instinctively know that integrity means something more than honesty — it also means self awareness and honest self-appraisal.

Integrity becomes the commitment to a vision and to one's deepest values. It is the courage to embrace honesty and to make tough choices and to forego what is easy and comfortable. Without integrity, you cannot really create or maintain trust within your organizational community.

I was faced with a defining moment in my career. For six months, I had been facilitating a cross-functional team of top leaders, with little progress. The name of the organization and the nature of the team's task are unimportant. What is important, at least to me, is that morning I stood at the front of the meeting room and said:

"I'm going to live one of my ground rules by being as open, honest, and direct as I know how. My experience is that we have been colluding to create boring, long, ineffective meetings. I acknowledge that we have made occasional choices in favor of higher effectiveness. But, generally, our meetings drain our life energy and make only a marginal difference.

I acknowledge my breakdown of participating in the collusion. I was, for a while, off purpose. I re-awakened to my purpose at the end of our last meeting. It was, frankly, one of the worst meetings I have ever participated in.

I will not collude with you to create meetings like that any more. My life energy is too precious to waste. Your life energy is too precious to waste.

So, here's my declaration.

I believe the process of life is growth. You're either growing, dying, or dead. There's only one of those states I want to be in. So, my intention, my purpose is to promote freedom, growth, and joy in every interaction, with every person, in every moment. In every moment I have conscious control over what I choose to believe and what I choose to do. And my job is to create space for others to observe what is happening in the moment and make their own conscious choices. It's what distinguishes me and my organization. Serving our highest purpose is more vital than any project team, any client, any amount of money.

I'm on purpose.
The next choice is yours."

Creating Trust

People follow leaders to extremes because they trust them. Creating trust is essential to good leadership and to the success of our organizations. According to Bennis, the main determinants of trust are reliability and constancy.

People will follow a leader if they trust this person and feel confident in his or her presence. People want to know that the leader will not abandon them in the middle of their journey. Bennis also suggests that positive changes require trust, clarity, and participation. People trust leaders who walk their talk and fulfill their commitments.

Curiosity, Daring, and Innovation

Leaders also are curious. They are innovators. They are audacious, adventurous and energetic. This is essential because leaders encourage their followers to discover new horizons, take risks, and make the required changes to pursue the dream.

Organizing Groups

An essential skill of the leader is coordinating a network of people. This talent is seen in theater directors, producers, military officers, and effective heads of many organizations. On the playground, the budding leader is the child who takes the lead in identifying what everyone will play, or the one who becomes team captain (Goleman). To improve this skill, we encourage you to take some risks and organize a transformation or process improvement team.

Simple Tactics

Following is a list of behaviors that you can use to lead others and work miracles in small and big ways:

- Listen while others talk in order to understand what they are saying.
- Paint vivid pictures of, and dramatize, your ideas.
- Celebrate the little victories.
- Share your enthusiasm, which will arouse the same in other people.
- Challenge yourself and others to stretch.
- Incorporate and give credit to others' ideas, thus fostering collaboration.
- Seek to understand and find solutions rather than confront.
- Share your passion for work, rather than manipulate people.
- Ask questions instead of making statements of truth.
- Admit mistakes quickly and emphatically.
- Recognize contributions, personal issues, and growth.
- Find creative ways to support the work of those around you.
- Invite others to be part of the creative process.
- See things from the other person's point of view.
- Show honest appreciation for the people surrounding you.
- Seek feedback frequently.
- Use encouragement when you give feedback.
- Be clear in your expectations.
- Spend time getting to know those you lead; learn from them.

SUMMARY POINTS

◆ Alignment begins with understanding your larger purpose, and it requires your conscious involvement in the strategic planning process.

◆ By matching individual energies with the organization's requirements, the probability of creating desired results improves.

◆ Creating individual and organizational vision alignment is a process in which individuals are called upon to take risks, be intellectually honest, and share openly with colleagues.

◆ Four steps to create individual and organizational vision alignment include:
  ◆ Step 1: Develop collective consciousness of personal visions.
  ◆ Step 2: Define organizational requirements for success.
  ◆ Step 3: Declare energy interests.
  ◆ Step 4: Ensure there is sufficient energy to achieve organizational requirements.

◆ When the planning process is designed to address the whole person, a more true and straightforward plan emerges; people see their connection and contribution.

QUESTIONS AND REFLECTIONS

What is my personal vision? My vision for my organization? The accepted vision for my organization?

How much alignment is there between my vision and the accepted one?

How much energy am I currently putting toward my organization's vision?

How much do I know about others' personal and organizational visions?

What could I start doing immediately to channel different individual energies (including my own) toward the organizational vision?

What is the risk of sharing personal visions within my organization? Am I willing to take such a risk?

Where do I have energy? Where do others have energy?

What is my best guess as to the balance of total energy within my organization versus the requirements for success?

What characteristics do I currently have that support leading with vision? Which ones do I need to develop?

Chapter 4

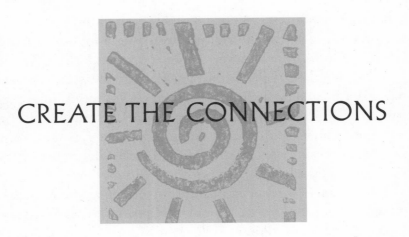

CREATE THE CONNECTIONS

"Separation leads to disintegration, and joining leads to miracles."
- Marianne Williamson

"Social psychologists tell us that we cannot truly be persons unless we interact with other persons. All life is interrelated, and all men are interdependent. And yet we continue to travel a road paved with the slippery cement of inordinate selfishness."
- Martin Luther King, Jr.

Y ou have the power to bring people together and help them build strong relationships. If you want to learn more about people and what makes relationships work, you are ready to strengthen your interpersonal insight. Interpersonal insight is the ability to understand what motivates people and how to work with them.

When you do not cultivate and enhance your interpersonal insight, you are less effective. This is because you do not accept and use all the information available from others. As a result, you miss opportunities in life and at work.

The quality of relationships at all organizational levels has a significant impact on performance. Fostering interpersonal insight makes all links in the organizational chain as strong as possible. High-performance relationships are the foundation of high-performance teams. And high-performance teams are the building blocks of high-performance organizations.

Effective work relationships are not created and maintained by chance. They require a conscious and disciplined approach that builds interpersonal insight within the organization's members. When interpersonal insight is high, people are able to analyze, engage and respond appropriately to others.

> *I recently took a "social/emotional intelligence" test on the Internet. I scored badly, not because I'm emotionally challenged, but because I never do well on standardized tests (NOTE: add this to Victim Stories in Chapter 2). Seriously, in taking the test, I think I got caught up in being right. In other words, it was all about me. That's the big thing I've learned when it comes to managing relationships - if I focus on myself first, I get one kind of result. If I focus on the other person first, a different, better kind of result. And when I remember to focus on that other person as a spirit housed in a body, I am truly a social/emotional genius!*

Facets of Interpersonal Insight

The core of interpersonal insight includes the capacity to appropriately discern and respond to other people's moods, temperaments, motivations, and desires. This chapter explores facets of interpersonal insight, which you must continuously cultivate. Interpersonal insight includes four abilities (Goleman, 1995):

- leadership;
- social analysis;
- relationship management; and
- conflict resolution.

As discussed in Chapter 3, *leadership* is the way you serve as a role model to other people, influencing their actions, shaping their decisions, and providing guidance to them. *Social analysis* is the ability to look into people's hearts and minds and understand their feelings, concerns, and ideas. *Relationship management* is how you connect with others and respond to them in a way that builds trust. *Conflict resolution* is used to prevent or resolve disputes while at the same time celebrating people's diversity.

People with interpersonal insight effectively lead and organize people; accurately read reactions and feelings; quickly connect with others; and can easily mediate social discord. These people can articulate the unspoken collective sentiment to guide a group toward its goals. They are the kind of people you like to be with because they are emotionally nourishing. They leave you in a good mood and uplifted. Their presence never drains your energy; instead it gives you energy.

The lifelong journey to interpersonal mastery requires continuous risk taking, practicing new behaviors and soliciting feedback from others. Remember the levels of effectiveness in Chapter 2? Just as risk taking, practice and feedback increase your self awareness, they are equally important for building your interpersonal effectiveness. Risks, practice, and feedback are necessary to master leadership, social analysis, relationship management, and conflict resolution.

LEARN TO LEAD

Chapter 3 is devoted to leadership. The ability to lead involves vision, passion, integrity, curiosity, risk taking and organizing. People want three things in a leader: vision, trustworthiness, and optimism. A leader is a person you will follow to a place you would not go by yourself. True leaders shape organizational culture and core values. A good leader invites whole people to show up in the workplace and taps into the vast power of their creative spirits. Leading also requires the ability to analyze social situations.

LEARN TO ANALYZE SOCIAL SITUATIONS

Interpersonal insight involves assessing people's feelings, motives, and concerns. This is called **social analysis** and is the ability to understand others' emotions, adopt their perspectives in order to see things from their points of view, and respect their personal differences. Goleman (1995) describes social analysis as a critical ability.

Social analysis includes feeling empathy; being a good listener and questioner; discerning between what someone says and does; and distinguishing between reactions and judgments. Cultivating this ability is another crucial step to interpersonal insight. If you take risks, practice new behaviors and seek feedback on your social analysis skills, you can:

- ◆ communicate better;
- ◆ improve your perception;
- ◆ take on others' perspectives;
- ◆ improve your listening abilities; and
- ◆ experience greater sensitivity to others' feelings.

Social analysis leads to rapport with others, rapport leads to intimacy, and intimacy leads to relationships. Relationships are the building blocks of our work communities. Even though it can be a challenge, establishing new relationships is rather easy when compared to managing relationships over time.

LEARN TO MANAGE RELATIONSHIPS

Any ongoing association between two or more individuals is a relationship. Relationships take diverse forms and have varied roots, such as affection, kinship, and work. Regardless of its nature, a relationship indicates two or more persons have established an ongoing connection.

The bond between people who are in relationship has unique properties, including a sense of history and a commitment to maintain the connection. People in relationship influence each other's thoughts, feelings, and behaviors. They expect to interact with each other in the future.

Relationships play an essential role in supporting and providing a context for most of our work environments. In fact, our workplaces are complex networks of relationships. The work that you sign up to do — whether functional, transformational, or crisis driven — is influenced by your connections to coworkers.

Skillful relationship management is critical to your personal and professional effectiveness. If you possess the ability to create and maintain connections with others, you are better equipped to be a team member, dependable partner, and good friend. At work, you are better postured to join forces with others in transforming your organization.

The nature of relationships has been widely studied and analyzed. For example, according to Chadwick and Jones (1976) relationships between people are like business transactions. Imagine interactions between people as having costs and benefits. Think of costs and benefits as things like status, money, love, services, goods, and information. So, the outcome of an interaction is defined as the benefit minus its cost. This suggests that you are drawn to relationships that maximize your desired outcomes.

Desired outcomes that people expect from you include feeling cared about and being respected. Therefore, managing relationships involves empathizing with other perspectives, acknowledging feelings, respecting differences, and constantly seeking truth in interactions. The focus is on understanding, maintaining and enhancing personal connections. Relationship management skills include:

- having a beginner's mind;
- being a good listener and questioner;
- being persuasive and allowing yourself to be persuaded;
- demonstrating assertiveness rather than anger or passivity;
- knowing the art of cooperation, conflict resolution, and compromise;
- distinguishing between what someone says or does and your own reactions.

Poor relationships are a primary driver of performance problems in organizations. Yet often there are few attempts to understand and resolve interpersonal tensions. As more organizations adopt team-based approaches, people must learn to effectively manage multiple relationships at work.

University faculty are not known for their ability to collaborate, share resources, or engage in innovative management practices. A senior faculty member asked me to facilitate and coach a team he was putting together. I hesitated, but he finally convinced me they were serious. What a pleasant surprise this became.

We put together an organization that crossed four colleges and six departments. The team has obtained research funding and conducted collaborative projects where none existed before. Individual team members have been recognized for excellence from their own colleges. How did this happen? Each of the six faculty members entered this team voluntarily. They were invited by colleagues, not administrators.

Even though two of the team members had some management related backgrounds, they all deferred process decisions to the facilitator or group consensus. To avoid partisanship, they asked me, the facilitator, to make their presentations to the administration so their plan would appear to be a team plan. They were looking for bigger pies, not bigger pieces. And finally, when the six of them united for common goals, their complimentary strengths created contagious levels of energy. They were fun to work with.

Managing Agreements and Breakdowns

Part of relationship management is how you approach agreements and breakdowns. Ultimately, performance around your agreements forms the basis of trust that others have for you. Therefore, your skill in making and managing agreements is critical to strong and lasting relationships.

When a breakdown in an agreement occurs, you must first acknowledge the breakdown. Many individuals do not take this important step and instead offer a flood of excuses. Without acknowledgement, conversation about the breakdown can come to a standstill and jeopardize the ensuing relationship.

Each party must go back to the original agreement and seek clarification. Things to check include: the nature of the agreement; what each party heard; and the definition of performance.

Following acknowledgment of a breakdown, a new understanding must be forged regarding future expectations. The new agreement is based upon lessons learned from the breakdown. In this way, you can grow from failed agreements and learn how to better manage future commitments.

Your cumulative record of agreements forms the essence of how people view you. How you approach and honor commitments is a defining dimension of your life. Over time, your ability to make and manage agreements will determine the strength of your relationships.

Your long-term challenge is to build sustainable relationships. Sustainable relationships are built upon managed agreements with your coworkers, partners, children, and friends.

Work Rules

Interpersonal insight can be greatly improved through the use of tools such as ground rules. Following are seven such rules that have been adopted by thousands of employees, from all walks of organizational life. These ground rules have proven to create rapid and sustainable results in the areas of personal effectiveness, relationship management, and organizational performance.

Because of their direct application to the work environment, we refer to them as "work rules." **Work rules** are principle-based guidelines for building interpersonal mastery and high-performance relationships. They are not esoteric, mysterious, or religious.

Work rules are self-evident and intuitive. They are based upon principles that govern human effectiveness. Principles such as these influence human growth and happiness and include:

- learning, growing, and risk-taking;
- making a difference and experiencing joy when doing it;
- taking responsibility for self, relationships, and community;
- doing what is right and being accountable at the highest level; and
- looking for ways to align and attune human spirits and energies.

Following is a set of seven work rules based upon these principles:

- ◆ Manage all agreements.
- ◆ Use open, honest and direct communication.
- ◆ Maintain a supportive environment.
- ◆ Maintain confidentiality.
- ◆ Stay focused and be prepared.
- ◆ Hold a proper attitude for learning.
- ◆ Be self-monitoring.

Manage all agreements.
Your cumulative record of agreements forms the essence of how others view you. So get clear on your commitments, make fewer of them, and keep the ones that you make. Seek to minimize the impact of any commitments that you choose to break by informing others in advance that you will not keep the agreement. If this is not possible, acknowledge breakdowns as soon as possible after the fact. Another thing that affects people's perceptions of you is how you communicate.

Use open, honest and direct communication.
Say what you think and feel to the people who you believe would benefit from your message. With respect to being open, be clear as opposed to sending hidden messages. On the matter of being honest, truthfully share your thoughts, ideas, and feelings. When it comes

to being direct, share your message with the person it is intended for as opposed to telling someone who you hope will pass it along. It is possible to be open, honest and direct while at the same time being supportive.

Maintain a supportive environment.

Recognize, encourage, and help people who take risks. Really listen to what others are saying. Help them in any way you can. Invite people to participate as opposed to excluding them. Give recognition to people who take risks. Honor people's privacy, which relates to confidentiality.

Maintain confidentiality.

Weigh carefully the potential consequences of quoting other people and spreading gossip. This means guarding against attribution and retribution. Attributing statements to others out of context can be misleading. Also remember that people who pay a price (receive retribution) for what they do or say will be shy about showing up as a whole person in the future. Maintaining confidentiality builds trust and puts people at ease to be creative, think outside the box, and get focused.

Stay focused and be prepared.

Define and understand what it means to be on purpose and remain there. Stay on the issues and topics. Being prepared can have many meanings, depending upon the situation. It can include getting rest, reviewing materials, and holding preparatory conversations. In meetings, do not take a vacation in your mind. It also helps to create a list of items that are "parked for later." This can keep meeting participants from getting caught up in tangential issues. Focus and preparation are proper behaviors for learning.

Hold a proper attitude for learning.
Remain open to, contribute to, and build upon new ideas. No matter what is said, stay open to the 1 percent possibility that a statement has value and that you can learn from it. Suspend judgment, seeking first to understand the message of the other person. A proper attitude for learning also requires self awareness, which means it is important to monitor yourself.

Be self-monitoring.
Place an imaginary video camera or mirror on yourself. View your behaviors and see how they play out. Continuously hold up the mirror to see your reflection. Then, make appropriate adjustments. This work rule is your reminder to continuously build your self awareness in order to expand Quadrant 2 of Johari's Window (discussed in Chapter 2).

When work rules are broken repeatedly, trust is lost. When used as a tool for managing relationships, work rules build a foundation for long-term trust.

Seek Feedback

If you want vision alignment in your organization, feedback is essential. Once purpose, vision, and goals are shared among individuals, the opportunity for each individual then becomes to gather feedback (input and observations) from others. Proactively seeking feedback is challenging and at the same time rewarding.

Seeking feedback expands Quadrant 2 of Johari's Window (what others know that you do not know about yourself). Unfortunately, people often wait for work relationships to become strained or damaged before making the effort to seek feedback. For clarity, let's call the person who asks for feedback "the seeker," and the person who provides feedback "the giver."

Interestingly enough, the feedback already exists in the giver's mind. All the seeker needs to do is ask for it. This is because people notice and remember details about other people's performance. People perceive whether or not others are moving forward. They notice behaviors and actions that create successes and failures.

Feedback is a precious gift. It is one gift that is okay to request. People love to give feedback but are sometimes fearful of creating hurt feelings by offering it. You should ask for feedback, as opposed to waiting for others to offer it. In this manner, your receptivity is clearly demonstrated, and it puts the giver at ease.

You should ask yourself two questions prior to seeking feedback:

- ◆ Do I want the honest observation, or just positive comments to build my ego?

♦ Am I prepared to receive the gift as offered, or do I intend to twist the giver's comments to fit a preconceived notion or position?

To share feedback objectively requires calmness and understanding. It demands honoring and caring for the seeker. Without respect by both parties for both roles, a feedback session can become a forum for unloading baggage and resentment. This can cause confusion and jeopardize the relationship.

If you are the giver, you have a big responsibility. To be a gift, feedback must be given with little or none of your baggage. To be helpful as a giver, you must check your ego. You must ask yourself if you are in a mental and emotional state to share feedback that is free of baggage and resentment.

As the giver you should also be aware of projection, which means unconsciously providing feedback that is more about your own strengths, weaknesses, and fears than about the seeker's. Your effectiveness at giving feedback is greatest when your self awareness is high. Exhibit A contains a proven way to effectively seek and share feedback.

Seeker: Would you give me some feedback?

Giver: My intention for giving you this feedback is...

(Giver states the purpose of giving the feedback. This provides a chance to check underlying motivation. Is the feedback honest and genuine? Is it dumping or projecting?)

          My experience of you is ...

(Giver shares personal experiences, not secondhand information or hearsay. The opportunity is to maintain objectivity.)

          In order to be more effective, I suggest you:
          Start...
(What could the person do to increase personal effectiveness?)

          Stop...
(Suggestions for stopping certain unhealthy or unproductive behaviors and actions to increase personal effectiveness.)

          Continue...
(List the things done by the person that are presently effective.)

Seeker: Thank you for the feedback.

(No comment of the accuracy of the observations is required since it is the point of view of the giver. Only acknowledge the gift of feedback.)

Exhibit A: The Feedback Exercise

Develop Trust

Trust is a foundational element of relationship management. Understanding, building, and enhancing trust with family, friends, and coworkers is challenging. And at the same time, trust is an essential element for transforming the workplace. The need in today's organizations to achieve a high level of cooperation and cohesion demands high levels of trust.

Results of cross-functional teams, virtual collaboration efforts, and extended supply systems vary widely in seemingly comparable organizations. Interpersonal skills are at the heart of these performance differences. Specifically, a contributor to different levels of performance, cited by leaders, is varying degrees of trust among individuals.

Vulnerability and Types of Trust

It is difficult to find a global definition of trust. Vulnerability is the common ground among the definitions of trust in the literature. For example, Rousseau (1998) views trust as a "psychological state comprising the intention to accept vulnerability based upon positive expectations of the intentions or behavior of another." For Zand (1997), trust is the willingness to increase vulnerability to another person. Different types of trust, or ways of extending vulnerability, include:

- ✦ **Deterrence-based trust** (Rousseau et al, 1998; Coutu, 1998) rests on the sanctions in place for abusing trust that would exceed any benefits from betrayal.
- ✦ **Calculus-based trust** (Rousseau et al, 1998) rests on the credible information about the trustee

regarding intentions and/or competence, and the fact that the trustee will benefit from his or her performance.

♦ **Relational trust** rises from "repeated interaction over time" between the two parties (Rousseau et al, 1998).

♦ **Institution-based trust** (Rousseau et al, 1998; McKnight et al, 1998) is based on the control systems and trust supports provided by institutional (organizational or social) culture and structure.

♦ **Knowledge-based trust** (McKnight et al, 1998; Coutu, 1998) rests on the fact that people get to know each other over time and a level of predictability is achieved.

♦ **Personality-based trust** (McKnight et al, 1998) is a natural tendency to trust, or distrust, that one will have developed during one's personal history, particularly childhood.

♦ **Cognition-based trust** (McKnight et al, 1998) is built on rapid cognition and first impressions.

♦ **Identification-based trust** (Coutu, 1998) is built on the empathy and shared values among the members of the same community or the same organization.

♦ **Conditional trust** (Jones and Georges, 1998) is sustained as long as the other party behaves appropriately, while **unconditional trust** is given without firm expectations.

Each of these types can be a step in the process of building trust. For example, Coutu (1998) sees the development of trust among virtual work teams as the succession of deterrence-based trust, knowledge-based trust, and finally, identification-based trust.

Capability, Commitment and Consistency

Trusting (or distrusting) behavior is driven by the beliefs we have about each other in three areas. These three components of trust include capability, commitment and consistency.

- **Capability** – The ability to produce results and to deliver performance. Does the other person have the skills to get the job done? You may trust a small boy's sincerity when he claims to be able to slam dunk a basketball, but you do not trust his capability to make it happen. You do not believe the child understands the "gravity" of the challenge. When an individual or team chooses a lofty goal, trust may be in question when the complexity or requirements of such an accomplishment are not well understood.

- **Commitment** – The concern that each party is perceived to have for the other. Does each party have the other's best interests in mind? When unforeseen problems arise or the agreement takes more effort than originally believed, does one still make it happen? Business partnerships often falter because the commitment was more to self interest than to the partnership.

- **Consistency** – Do the parties demonstrate agreement between their words and their actions? Over time do they live up to their spoken words, their pronouncements? Being a "person of your word" requires living in integrity. Integrity is not a faucet that can be turned on or off. Integrity obligates you to adopt a certain mindset, which includes consistency among beliefs, spoken agreements, and actions. Coherence among thoughts, words and deeds is a way of life for the person of integrity.

You must establish trust in order to get people aligned (Bennis, 1989). To build trust, you must act in ways that influence people's perceptions of your capability, commitment and consistency. These are the building blocks of sustainable trust. Achieving results in differing circumstances will drive a belief in capability. Acting in an unselfish manner toward another will impact perceptions of your commitment to the relationship. Demonstrating integrity, having your deeds follow your words, will build others' confidence in your consistency.

Additional Factors
Additionally, trust is built and sustained by four things (Shaw, 1997; Kohen, 1997):
+ Leadership
+ Infrastructure
+ Culture
+ Risk

A leader shows the way to build a living and self-sustaining organization. The leader's behaviors and attitudes are a reference for her followers. For this reason the leader must act in a trustworthy way, and enhance trust in the organization through levels and functions.

The organization's infrastructure must be simple enough to be understood by everyone. Accountabilities and roles need to be clearly defined. Communication within the culture should facilitate information sharing and collaboration. The controls necessary to avoid abuse or misuse of employees' power must not restrain creativity and energy. Armed with a compelling vision and solid ground rules, the leader sets the organization's focus on building value with all its surroundings. This is challenging work.

It is a risk for leaders to step out in front and declare their intention to build a great organization. Risk is often associated with trust. For Kohen (1997), trust or distrust emerges when people perceive potentially undesirable outcomes. In other words, if you trust someone, you accept the risk that this person might either fail to meet your expectations or betray you.

The growth of trust in a relationship is a reciprocal process of risk taking in which both individuals allow themselves to be vulnerable. One type of risk that is highly effective in building trust is to act in ways that put the other's needs before your own. By taking risks that expose you to potential disappointment and hurt, you are able to signal your intentions and thus furnish the other with the type of evidence needed to reduce uncertainty regarding your motives.

Intriguingly, as the cycle of reciprocal risk-taking escalates, reassurance and confidence increase. It is fairly simple: trust is born from trusting acts. To gain trust, a person must trust others. You can extend behavioral trust by taking risks that expose your weaknesses, fears, concerns, and hopes.

Subjective and Behavioral Trust

True consensus on a definition of trust remains elusive. However, social psychologists have agreed on two things: Trust can be viewed 1) as a subjective state of being, and 2) as trusting behavior.

Subjective trust is a readiness or predisposition to trust others. It is the process of evaluating others as worthy of trust, given the appropriate circumstances. It is described as a state of subjective certainty, confidence, or faith that some other person, upon whom we must depend, will not act in ways that might bring us painful consequences. If one thinks of trust on a scale of 1-10, a rating of subjective trust might be voiced as, "On a scale of 1-10, I trust you at a 6."

Behavioral trust is subjective trust put into action. This is the observable behavior of an individual who has confident expectations about the benevolence of another's motives and intentions. A central tenet is that trusting behavior typically involves placing yourself in a position of potential vulnerability relative to another. While subjective trust represents a feeling of confidence in others' motives, behavioral trust is the resulting action you take based on your level of subjective trust.

While theorists view these two faces of trust as conceptually distinct, they are intimately linked in people's real-life experiences. Whether or not you choose to engage in trusting behavior in any particular situation is based upon your appraisal of the other's trustworthiness. In other words, it is your degree of certainty or faith that the person to be trusted is unselfishly and charitably motivated (Manstead & Hewstone, 1996).

One way to extend behavioral trust is the trust exercise. Similar to the feedback exercise, it involves sharing honest observations. Normally it is done with an agreement to exchange perceptions regarding trust with another. The exercise can begin with either party. Exhibit B contains the trust exercise.

Giver: What I base trust on is...
(Given there are different definitions and beliefs of trust, offer a short statement of how you view trust, including the elements of trust.)

My level of trust for you is...
(Use a 1-10 scale of trust, with 1 being extremely low trust, and 10 being extremely high trust.)

What makes me trust you at this level is...
(Share characteristics and/or behaviors promote trust in the relationship.)

What keeps me from trusting you at a 10 is...
(Share characteristics and/or behaviors that undermine trust in the relationship.)

What I intend to do to build trust with you is...
(Provide actions you will take, if any, to move toward a more trusting relationship with the seeker.)

Seeker: Thank you for being honest.

Exhibit B: Trust Exercise

People sometimes consider the trust exercise to be a huge risk. In some group experiences, participants have even joked about getting sweaty palms. Even if you have some initial apprehension, the outcome of the trust exercise to be well worth the risk.

If you openly discuss the mutual level of trust you have with a person, the relationship becomes more honest. As with the feedback exercise, the trust exercise reveals how others perceive us in areas that otherwise would not be shared. Again, this helps expand Quadrant 2 of Johari's Window, what others know about us that we do not know about ourselves.

An increased level of trust between people is a natural outcome of sharing personal thoughts and impressions. Even in trusting relationships, friction occurs. In these instances, it is important to know how to resolve conflict in a way that builds the relationship.

LEARN TO MEDIATE CONFLICT

Masters of interpersonal relations are frequently excellent mediators who prevent conflicts or resolve those that flare up. Mediation is one of the most difficult elements of interpersonal mastery because people are reluctant to deal with conflict. Conflict resolution requires hard work and perseverance. The key is to move beyond conflict and to channel spiritual energy into the co-creation of results.

Many people perceive conflict as a negative experience. They fear conflict because it means something has gone wrong in their relationship. Others deny conflict because they assume someone will get hurt or lose power.

Some individuals avoid conflict because they see it as a hopeless exercise, in which each party will fight for position or ego. In fact, conflict resolution can help build organizational community. It sets the stage for a disciplined approach to co-creation and transformation.

Weeks (1992) promotes "Eight Essential Steps to Conflict Resolution" which are:

- Create an effective atmosphere.
- Clarify perceptions.
- Focus on individual and shared needs.
- Build shared positive power.
- Look to the future, then learn from the past.
- Generate negotiating options.
- Develop "do-ables" – the stepping-stones to action.
- Make and manage mutual-benefit agreements.

Following is a brief explanation of each step:

Step 1: Create an Effective Atmosphere

Creating an environment for conflict resolution involves personal preparation (mental, physical, and spiritual). You must establish the right timing, identify an appropriate location, and know the objectives of the initial meeting. This is important because mental attitude and preparedness influence the outcome. Rather than jumping into an intense conflict resolution process, establish the groundwork for effective interaction, maximize communication, and emphasize the positive aspects of all parties. Also choose a non-threatening and spirit-enhancing place. Finally, encourage and empower all parties to see their own connections to the conflict.

Step 2: Clarify Perceptions

Perceptions are the lenses through which you see yourself, others, your relationships, and your situation. Perceptions exert a huge influence over your personality, your way of dealing with things, your behaviors, and your attitudes. Perceptions play a major role in the causes of conflict and in the way you deal with it. As part of conflict resolution, you must help all parties clarify: 1) perceptions of the conflict; 2) perceptions of the self; and 3) perceptions of the conflict partner.

Step 3: Focus on Individual and Shared Needs

Unless the needs of each party in the relationship and the needs of the relationship are dealt with, the relationship itself cannot realize its full potential. You should not, however, confuse needs ("must haves") with desires ("nice to haves"). The key is to create an understanding of each party's shared and individual needs.

Step 4: Build Shared Positive Power

Develop and engage positive power to resolve conflicts effectively. Power consists of the right attitudes, perceptions, beliefs and behaviors that empower people and groups to act or perform effectively. Positive power does not mean winning against and weakening the conflict partner. Positive power is win-win, specifically promoting the constructive capabilities of all parties in the conflict. It is shared positive power that actually constructs the process and moves it toward effective resolution. This shared power is stronger than individual power. Shared positive power creates the energy needed to achieve effective resolution.

Step 5: Look to the Future, then Learn from the Past

Every conflict has a past, present, and future, and resolving conflicts effectively requires dealing with all three. The past provides an experiential foundation for the present and the future. The present brings past memories into new light. The present and the future are inseparable, as we create the future in the present. The past can impede conflict resolution if the parties do not overcome frustrations and address previous problems. Yet the past can also help if the parties choose to learn from it. Therefore, facilitating understanding of the history or origins of the conflict is crucial. If people want to maintain a relationship, they have to focus on what can be done in the present to ensure all parties get what they need in the future. Forgiveness of past transgressions may become crucial, because without trust there is no basis on which to build the future. Focusing on the present and future engages all parties to stress common beliefs, benefits, and goals.

Step 6: Generate Negotiating Options

Generating negotiating options can often break through the preconceived limitations brought into the conflict resolution process. Generating options provides choices of means, goals, and techniques to resolve conflicts and improve relationships. As a mediator you should move beyond preconceived answers and look more deeply to find alternative commonalties.

Step 7: Develop "Do-ables," the Stepping Stones to Action

Do-ables are actions that: meet shared needs; do not favor one party; require mutual participation; and have a good chance of being accomplished. Do-ables are successful acts that meet some individual and shared needs, and depend on positive and shared power. In dealing with conflict, people often fail to build the conflict resolution process on stepping stones or do-ables. They think they know the desired outcome and delude themselves into leaping straight for it. If you can help the parties focus on mutually beneficial do-ables, they will discover they can work together and feel more confident about resolving the conflict.

Step 8: Make Mutual-Benefit Agreements

Once you have built a structure for relationship improvement and effective conflict resolution, the eighth and final step is developing mutual-benefit agreements to resolve specific conflicts. Mutual-benefit agreements are built on do-ables. These agreements do not really end the conflict but actually begin an improved process to deal with the differences. These eight steps can be repeated as often as needed. Along with leadership, social analysis, and interpersonal insight, these eight steps to conflict resolution help build the high-performance relationships necessary for a high-performance organization. In all cases, you want to create and maintain as many healthy connections as possible.

I had committed to work with a group for nine days to form a highly effective team. It was an outdoor venue that used backpacking, canoeing, and rock climbing to build relationships. After about five days, the group's interpersonal dynamics turned ugly. They had the skills they needed to accomplish tasks and work together, but they had not committed to working together. Members were short-tempered and reactive with each other. Everyone seemed to be on edge. It was a critical time for the group—either they would get past it and move forward, or they would melt down into self-serving bickering with little hope of reconciliation.

The next event was a 500 foot rock face climb. They had practiced the knots, safety commands, and climbing techniques. In every "technical" way, they were ready. But spirits were all over the map. A few were excited, some were ho-hum, and some were quiet and non-committal. But one person—a 55 year old woman in a group of 22 to 55 year olds, a woman whose cheery disposition and can-do attitude had gotten the group through some tough times thus far—assembled the group late in the day before the ascent to wish them well and to say she was not going to climb.

A shock wave rippled through the group. At first they thought she must be joking. As she explained that she didn't think she could do it, that it was beyond her ability to achieve, encouragement began spilling out of the others. As dusk settled in, each person in turn spoke of the meaningful support she had offered them at crucial times. As team members spoke, the circle closed tighter around the candle in the middle. By the time each person said their piece, the feeling in the group was that they could levitate her to the top of the mountain. She agreed to try ...

> *In that magic moment, the group was transformed from a collection of individuals with different motives and means of achieving them to a focused, high-energy, and caring team. They remained that way. Compassion was the key.*

IT ALL BOILS DOWN TO CONNECTIONS

Following are ways to create and sustain connections:

- Honor other people.
- Extend and build trust.
- Express love for other people.
- Solicit support for your own growth.
- Listen with the intention to understand.
- Share your passion and personal vision.
- Support other people's growth journey.
- Understand others and what they are about.
- Show sincere interest in others and the path they are taking in life.

All in all, people want to feel connected to each other and to something bigger than them. The four facets of interpersonal insight (leadership, social analysis, relationship managment, and conflict resolution) can help you create and sustain important connections. When it's all said and done, organizational transformation is not possible without healthy individuals and healthy relationships. With this foundation, you are ready to adopt a discipline to transform your workplace.

SUMMARY POINTS

◆ High-performance relationships are the foundation of high-performance teams, and high-performance teams are the building blocks of high-performance organizations.

◆ Interpersonal Insight is the ability to understand what motivates people and how to work with them.

◆ The four facets of interpersonal insight are: leadership, social analysis, relationship management, and conflict resolution.

◆ Leadership involves guiding vision, passion, integrity, curiosity, risk taking and organizing.

◆ Seven work rules that promote interpersonal insight are:
   ◆ Manage all agreements.
   ◆ Use open, honest and direct communication.
   ◆ Maintain a supportive environment.
   ◆ Maintain confidentiality.
   ◆ Stay focused and be prepared.
   ◆ Hold a proper attitude for learning.
   ◆ Be self-monitoring.

◆ Three components of trust are capability, commitment and consistency.

QUESTIONS AND REFLECTIONS

What is my ability to intuit other people's actions and motives?

What barriers keep me from looking inside other people?

How do I typically manage agreements and breakdowns?

Where is my opportunity to improve how I manage agreements and breakdowns?

Do I seek feedback? How much am I willing to accept?

What are my issues about people "finding me out"?

Do I know to what level my coworkers trust me?

What is my intention to build trust with my coworkers?

Do I lead by example when it comes to managing relationships? If so, how? In not, why?

How do I usually handle conflict?

In what ways can I improve my approach to conflict resolution?

Do I lead by example when it comes to managing conflict? If so, how? If not, why?

Chapter 5

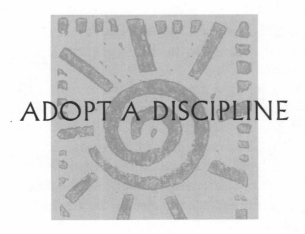

ADOPT A DISCIPLINE

"To play with passion requires discipline. There is no other way to generate the tireless energy that passion runs on. You set high standards and you hold to them."

- Gay Hendricks and Kate Ludeman

An unaligned organization wastes energy! So, adopt a discipline to create alignment. Chapters 1-4 showed you how to heighten self awareness and interpersonal insight. Now, learn to construct a transformation plan that leverages self awareness and interpersonal insight to generate alignment at all levels of your organization.

Associates of an unaligned organization may work hard, but their efforts are inefficient, like the scattered rays of a light bulb. On the other hand, when a group is aligned, a resonance develops, like the coherent light of a laser (Senge, 1990). Common direction, energy, vitality, harmony and spirit emerge in an aligned environment.

Members of aligned communities are interdependent and share a common purpose and vision. Individuals do not sacrifice their personal interests to the larger community vision. Instead, personal intentions build organizational vision.

Empowered people are the life force of an aligned workplace community. However, with little or no alignment, empowerment can result in confusion and disorder. Therefore, it is important to choose a discipline that both empowers and aligns people.

Your transformation process must build a solid plan. It must also promote self awareness, build community, and inspire dedication to making the change.

Dynamics of Community Building

In *A Different Drum*, M. Scott Peck (1988) describes four phases of community:

1) **Pseudocommunity-** In pseudocommunity, group members pretend to exhibit community traits by being polite and avoiding disagreement. They display avoidance and deny that individual differences exist.

2) Chaos- In chaos, differences are encouraged and exposed. Only now, instead of trying to hide or ignore them, the group attempts to obliterate them. Underlying the attempts to heal and convert others are the motives to make everyone normal and to win, as the members fight over whose norm might prevail.

3) Emptiness- Emptiness is the stage when members cleanse themselves of barriers to real communication. In this stage, preconceptions, prejudices, and the need to heal, convert, fix, and control are released.

4) Community- Community begins to form as the group transitions out of emptiness. Ideologies and theologies must be suspended long enough to hear others. Once these barriers are removed, community is achieved.

Marvin Weisbord (1987) explains the dynamics of transformation in a different way with his Four-Room Apartment model. The Four-Room Apartment looks at individual emotional states associated with change. As people experience different levels of group or organizational community, they enter different rooms of this apartment. Moving from room to room of the apartment is a normal part of the community-building process:

1) **Contentment**- In the room of contentment, a group member feels good about himself or herself and about the current situation. This room is comfortable and, at the same time, not very challenging.

2) **Denial**- In the room of denial, there is little or no admission that things have become challenging or that the change is difficult. The individual does not see that there are any opportunities to seize or any problems to solve.

3) **Confusion**- The room of confusion is visited as the need for the change becomes a reality. The individual realizes that much uncertainty and ambiguity are part of the transformation process and is not sure which way to turn. Confusion often results in some kind of personal catharsis or insight.

4) **Renewal**- The room of renewal is the room of breakthroughs. Development and growth bring renewal for the individual, who often leaves the room of renewal to revisit the room of contentment.

The dynamics of transformation occur simultaneously at two levels: individual and organizational. This multiple level transformation is necessary for work miracles to flourish. Another requisite is to move the organization's members to a creation mode of behavior and away from a strictly reaction mode.

CREATION vs. REACTION

It is difficult to move individuals and whole organization from reaction to creation and renewal. It is like moving from being *at effect* to being *at cause*. Reaction and creation are polar opposites, and occur at both the individual and organizational levels. Figures 10a and 10b illustrate individual and organizational Creation Journeys and Reaction Curves.

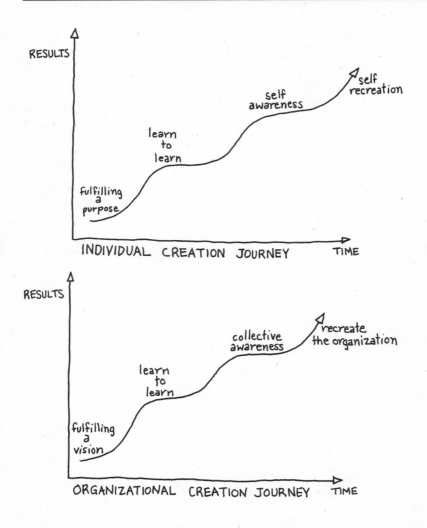

Figure 10a: Creation Journeys

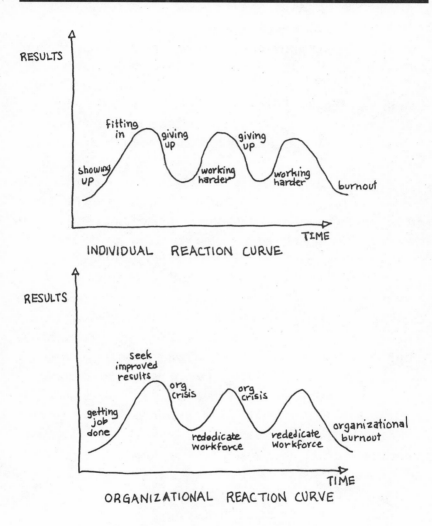

Figure 10b: Reaction Curves

Individual Reaction Curves

Often, just showing up at work is 80 percent of the job. *Showing Up* is the first step in the Individual Reaction Curve (Figure 10b). However, we would ask, "What is your intention in showing up? How does it relate to your life's purpose?" Some level of result has been accomplished in the first step and feeling secure enough to move forward, the individual reaches for more.

For many people, the workplace satisfies a social need — the need for affiliation, interaction, and engagement. Thus, *Fitting In* is important and is the second step in the Individual Reaction Curve. Here again, the questions arise, "What is your intention in fitting in? How does it relate to your life's purpose?"

By and large, today's workplace does not invite the whole person to be present. Given this, social interaction at work tends to be typically inauthentic and manipulated. Activities undertaken in the name of social expression — casual Fridays, group lunches, teambuilding exercises, and one-on-ones with the boss — often perpetuate a state of pseudocommunity.

The result is a carefully orchestrated façade and a collusion of niceties to maintain the appearance of organizational cohesion. In contrast, imagine a deeper level of social engagement in the workplace. Visualize an intimate conversation at work during which you relate one of the following:

- a recent spiritual insight;
- your deepest fears;
- what gives you joy.

For many, this type of interaction is inconceivable. In today's organizations, it seems an implicit wall of separation exists between the real self and the work self. A workplace contrived to accommodate partial people results in muted expression, lost connection, and lowered productivity.

Giving Up is a consequence. It manifests in "just-going-through-the-motions" behaviors. In this robotic state, people first languish, then wither as they mechanically execute their jobs. Disappointed by low personal effectiveness, the self edict becomes, "If I work harder to drive productivity and meaning into work, this situation will change. I will try to fit in with the flow and build something out of this work life."

Out of frustration and anger, a commitment is made to *Working Harder* at driving productivity and meaning into the job. But working harder does not work, the first time, second time, or ever. Too many talented individuals are running on an imaginary treadmill, working harder and getting nowhere. Giving up represented a temporary set back initially, but now a pattern is developed.

Unable to reach esprit by working harder, giving up is revisited over and over again until *Burnout* occurs. Check for blank eyes, a lack of physical energy, and a scarcity of enthusiasm. These are all signs that the individual, with help from the organization, has chosen the life of a zombie.

Organizational Reaction Curves

Like individuals, organizations exhibit reactionary patterns. Organizations do not live and breathe on their own; rather they reflect and magnify the intentions, behaviors, and mindsets of their leaders. The Organizational Reaction Curve (Figure 10b) is a model of leadership ineffectiveness.

In the reaction mode, the organization emphasizes *Getting the Job Done*. Whether to build ships, sell pizzas, or educate students, each organization exists to get a specific job done, to convert inputs to outputs. In an age of unparalleled competition and economic uncertainty, just getting the job done is no longer sufficient. Doing the job faster, cheaper, with fewer resources and higher-quality results is the requirement for survival. Improved results require individual, team, and organizational spirit and creativity.

Seeking Improved Results is the next step for the organization. But the workers' spirits are often left at the door. The consequence is failure to significantly generate improved, sustainable results. Unable to produce a breakthrough, the organization falters.

Less than expected financial and/or operational results precipitate an *Organizational Crisis.* To ensure employees understand the immediate danger of not changing and growing, management delivers motivational speeches, followed by a directive to *Rededicate the Workforce* to the same, unmet goals.

Not sure what to do, other than apply more effort and appear progressive, management declares the workforce must work smarter. However, with the same people, thinking the same way, with the same level of spiritual consciousness, the same results are produced.

The ultimate result is *Organizational Burnout.* Check for the lack of vibrancy when you walk in the door, the feel of imprisonment, and cynicism. These are all signs that the organization and the individuals within it have chosen to exist in a reaction mode.

The alternative is to move to the offensive and choose a creative stance to both an individual and organizational future. Making the shift from reaction to creation requires continuous focus and commitment. It is an unceasing process of exploration and renewal.

Individual Creation Journeys

The Individual Creation Journey (Figure 10a) begins with *Fulfilling a Purpose.* The Individual Development Document and the expanded Life Plan both call upon a declaration of life purpose (see Chapter 2). With an understanding of life purpose, showing up anywhere, at anytime becomes an expression of being on purpose.

Seeking meaning and placing work in the context of this meaning provides the spirit growing room. In other words, time spent at work is consistent with an individual's life purpose when on the creation journey. A person would not just land at work, but rather would choose work to reveal the nature of their purpose.

Moreover, the creation journey entails *Self-Awareness* and *Self-Recreation.* These words resonate with many and once introduced they are readily understood and used. However, not everyone who adopts the language is willing to commit to action and maintain long-term discipline.

An individual's creation journey calls for an honest internal dialogue. Once in the experience of working with life purpose in our mind's forefront, daily happenings deliver opportunities to learn. Honest answers to difficult questions expand self awareness:

- ◆ Why do I do the things I do in the workplace?
- ◆ Why do I get drawn into petty disagreements and expend so much of my life's energy on trivial matters?
- ◆ When I just try harder, why can't I accomplish something that lasts?
- ◆ When I'm joyful at work, what in me created it?
- ◆ When my relationships flourish, what are the common elements?

By moving into Self Awareness, you can then consciously choose to change nonproductive behaviors. From that stance, Self-Recreation becomes a reality. It is a unique ability we have, to remake ourselves. Our mind and spirit, equipped with a defined purpose, are able to change behaviors and thus, produce different results.

Organizational Creation Journeys

Just as miracles begin with individuals recreating themselves, workplace community becomes possible only when a critical mass of people possess high self awareness and alignment of their life's purpose to work choices. An organization filled with individuals engaged in self awareness and self-recreation has the capacity to work miracles. The Organizational Creation Journey (Figure 10a) begins with *Fulfilling a Vision.*

A collective vision postures the organization to build or create the environment, not just react in a survival mode. And as the organization moves forward with its purposeful work, daily happenings offer the chance to *Learn to Learn.* Can the organization, the collective community, learn from its experiences? This is a new skill for most organizations.

And in the case of the individual, it requires a self-examination that at times can be painful. Based upon discovered learnings, a level of *Collective Awareness* emerges. The organization as a whole develops the ability to assess progress toward a joint vision and without blame, determine corrective responses to move forward.

With this awareness in force the organization can choose to change its actions and thus, *Recreate the Organization.* Following recreation, the learning opportunity presents itself again, and the journey continues. A self-sustaining organization filled with collective spirit materializes. One of the opportunities for such an organization to seize is effective implementation.

IMPLEMENTATION IMPERATIVE

When examining the effectiveness of change initiatives, major problems appear not in their design but in implementation. Many times we look at an organization's most recent strategic plan and hear leaders criticize the quality and construction of the plan. These criticisms are often without merit.

Why? Because it was unrealistic to assess effectiveness when the plan had not been implemented. Leaders, middle managers, and employees had not committed to the plan, so implementation became haphazard at best. The same people who had exclaimed the plan would produce desired results had not followed through with executing the plan. These were good, smart people. They wanted to improve the organization.

What happened? Despite contrary pronouncements, change is not about having a desire and employing world-class tools to facilitate or drive results. Each organization is comprised of people with distinct relationships. So, to change the organization, a critical mass of people must heighten their self awareness and optimize how they relate with each other. Without these individual and interpersonal changes, neither the teams nor the organization can evolve.

Previous chapters discuss how, with the power of intention, personal and group transformations lay the groundwork for organizational transformation. Intention is critical in implementation of organizational improvement initiatives. Therefore, a transformation plan must reflect individual intentions. This means individuals must at least have a vision and a purpose.

When the concept of individual and group intention is firmly employed in the process, work miracles are in sight. The challenge is discovering a transformation process that allows people to fully employ personal energy and at the same time, align with others to create something extraordinary. Fortunately, ways do exist to plan change in diverse and large groups, and the body of knowledge on "how to" is growing rapidly. You can take advantage of collective knowledge gained to date by adopting a discipline such as the Transformation Cycle.

TRANSFORMATION CYCLE

Transformation must occur at all levels, and involve a creation mindset. Transformation implementation is governed by our intentions. Therefore, the process must acknowledge and use the power of intention. *The Transformation Cycle* facilitates alignment at all levels of the organization.

The Transformation Cycle produces individual and organizational Creation Journeys, which lead to improvement. The Transformation Cycle has worked in many settings. It evolved from twenty years of research and field testing. It integrates our collective knowledge and experience, building upon the earlier work of Sink, Deming, Senge, Kilmann, Weisbord, Peck, Bennis, Covey, Hammer and other organizational change leaders.

The Transformation Cycle has been used successfully in public and private sector organizations. It provides a framework for people to chart their course and that of the organization to navigate the turbulent and unpredictable whitewaters of change. The cycle integrates multidisciplinary methods for improving performance.

It addresses the missing link between individual empowerment and organizational performance improvement. At the same time, it puts solid management and industrial engineering tools to use. An extended creation community is the heart of this discipline for transforming the workplace.

A sound transformation process engages and involves the whole system. Command-and-control gives way to shared visioning. Personal initiatives become common goals. The process gathers a large representation of the system together to plan the organization's transformation.

Barbara Bunker and Billie Alban (1997) share characteristics of a process such as The Tranformation Cycle in *Large Group Interventions* including:

- ◆ ownership, commitment, alignment and speed are produced during the process;
- ◆ access to a critical mass of information enriches the change strategy; and
- ◆ creation of synergy is accomplished that leads to more innovative change.

In the last few decades many models have appeared that promised absolute performance breakthroughs. Countless computer-enhanced presentations impress audiences. Yet, despite the new, improved, modernized, revised, and enhanced approaches, nothing really seems to change in organizations. The people in organizations simply nod their heads and let new efforts die.

What is the missing ingredient? It is the spirit of community. Lack of community ensures difficulty and even failure. Without community, no improvement effort will succeed in the long term. Organizations require a firm foundation of trust and common ground to build community.

Embarking on an improvement process before establishing trust and common ground can result in a minimum payoff for your investment. If you do not take time to establish trust, surface the differences among people, and build community, any change or improvement effort is hampered as people play out their own (often unrevealed) goals, fears, concerns, beliefs, and prejudices. Therefore, the discipline of change must address these issues.

The Transformation Cycle has the following characteristics:

- ◆ Involves the extended organizational system.
- ◆ Focuses on improving individual effectiveness.
- ◆ Fosters relationships among members of the organization.
- ◆ Creates shared clarity about current reality and desired results.
- ◆ Sequences improvement activities that foster discipline and momentum.
- ◆ Integrates the management of interdependent organizational subsystems.

Figure 11 illustrates *The Transformation Cycle*. It includes traditional components of strategic planning, such as assessing and diagnosing the organization, defining a mission and vision, and identifying improvement objectives. Additionally, this large-scale transformation approach focuses on building commitment to the plan, managing implementation, aligning individuals and teams toward common objectives, and creating community to make the plan happen. The components of *The Transformation Cycle* include:

- Situation Appraisal
- Formation of the Transformation Design and Leadership Teams
- Transformation Design
- All-Hands Information Sharing
- Creating Alignment to Maximize Performance Pre-Work
- Creating Alignment to Maximize Performance Session
- Implementation Management
- Visible Results System
- Review Process
- Advance and Renewal Session
- Ongoing Education, Training and Development

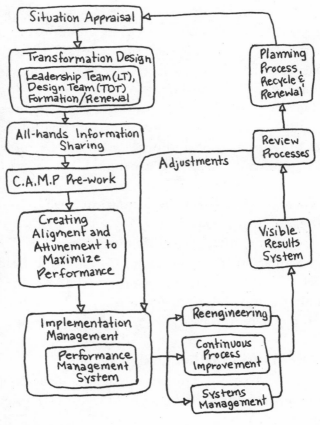

Ongoing:
Targeted Education, Training, and Development at all levels.

Figure 11: The Transformation Cycle

Situation Appraisal

The Transformation Cycle begins with a comprehensive organizational appraisal. Because organizations are engaged in continuous improvement, this appraisal targets the organization's effectiveness with change and attainment of its stated objectives. The assessment consists of written documentation, face-to-face interviews with top management, and diagonal sampling of the workforce. The information is evaluated and the summary of findings shared. An example of the situation appraisal format is in Appendix B.

Formation of the Transformation Design and Leadership Teams

Two teams integral to driving the transformation are the Transformation Design Team (TDT) and the Leadership Team (LT). Both are chartered teams. Generic elements of a team charter can be found in Appendix C. These teams play unique and different roles.

The Transformation Design Team

The TDT is responsible for designing, developing, and managing the transformation effort. This team is composed of the chief architects and engineers of the change. Their role is to detail strategies required to make the desired future state a reality. They recommend interventions, the formation of task teams, and often detail the planning front.

The TDT's role does not require their presence "out in front" of the organization, but rather behind the scenes. They recommend the course of action to the LT, relying upon the

LT to lead the effort. The leadership team is the "out in front" team, giving directions to implement the change. This is not the TDT's role, and confusion can be created if the TDT appears to be leading the transformation effort versus designing the transformation itself.

The TDT is a chartered team. Its sponsor is the LT, and the duration of its existence can be open or have an ending date. Members have the common trait of being systemic thinkers, able and desiring to see the whole picture.

Instead of random improvement projects and programs of the week, the TDT offers the organization the possibility to have a cohesive plan to transform the organization into a more effective and efficient vehicle for achieving defined outcomes. It is common for TDTs to initially meet once per week or once every two weeks. Later, monthly meetings are more common. In effective teams, much of the work is done outside of the team meeting.

The Leadership Team

The Leadership Team leads the organization through the transformation. It relies upon the TDT to make recommendation and accomplish much of the detailed planning of specific initiatives. The LT provides the TDT with guidance and direction. The LT sponsors the TDT's efforts. The leadership team's unique contribution is direction and guidance to the organization.

The LT is a standing team that does not disband. The LT is chartered and the sponsor is usually the leader of the organization or business unit. The leadership team is a decision and advisory team. The formal leader decides upon the areas of decision-making open to the LT. The use of a decision-making matrix by the leader is prudent, clarifying the role of the LT considering particular subject matters.

Transformation Design

This step lays out how the organization will establish an infrastructure to support the transformation. Here, you compare the ideal situation with the current reality, as observed and documented by the situation appraisal. The objective of the transformation design is to outline the necessary steps to close the gap between the ideal and the current situation. This is the initial plan concerned with engineering a recreated organization. Areas of concentrated effort are determined, along with timetables.

Change efforts or initiatives already underway are incorporated in the transformation design. Building on already existing and productive efforts is wise stewardship of the organizational energies. The transformation plan addresses transformational issues on the multiple levels, outlining the process to achieve the same.

All-Hands Information Sharing

People in organizations are usually afraid and/or suspicious of change efforts, and rightly so. People's reluctance increases as an initiative is launched. In many cases, it results from an authentic and understandable fear of the unknown. Or the reluctance is forthcoming because this is a recognizable road to failure.

Sharing sessions are scheduled to inform the organization stakeholders what will happen in the future with respect to The Transformation Cycle. In especially large organizations, this has been accomplished by using the formal site leadership with video representation from top management. These sessions are scheduled prior to the CAMP session.

The objective is to draw a map of the transformation journey and communicate the rationale behind the transformation. These sessions highlight why satisfaction with the status quo is not an option and why the organization and its stakeholders must change. Leadership articulates its commitment to the improvement process, describe expectations of and benefits, and provides a transformation change roadmap.

CAMP Pre-Work

CAMP (Creating Alignment to Maximize Performance) is a large group intervention. It is the intervention aimed at creating the energy, detailed planning and community required to transform the organization. It is done in such a manner that individual transformation is addressed.

Prior to the CAMP intervention, certain tasks are assigned to participants. Although pre-work for CAMP varies by each organization's need, readings are given, targeted at each of the four transformation cornerstones, discussed in Chapter 1.

Often, the Individual Development Document (IDD), described in Chapter 2 is given to participants to complete their first version. Some groups are requested to share their written IDDs with team members. In this process, an individual can articulate vision and goals. During the CAMP session, the individual will be ready to test the alignment of his or her vision and goals against those of the organization.

This component of the cycle initiates integration of self awareness into the organizational transformation. Other CAMP pre-work assignments may include identifying recommended actions based on the situation appraisal, identifying key performance indicators, conducting a self-assessment by the leadership team, or reading background articles.

CAMP Session

CAMP is a five-day, off-site session. It is a focused and intensive experience that stretches participants in the four Transformation Cornerstones: 1) self awareness, 2) interpersonal insight, 3) change mechanisms, and 4) requirements for success. We encourage broad stakeholder participation in CAMP, including key suppliers, customers, top management and a diagonal slice of the organization. For more details about CAMP, see Appendices D and E. Although each CAMP is different, all CAMP agendas are designed to:

- Create alignment (the degree to which people are working toward common organizational goals so individual intentions are clear and focused in the same direction);

- Develop attunement (the degree to which people work collaboratively so there is shared responsibility for the welfare of the entire system);

- Introduce mechanisms to develop a transformation plan;

- ◆ Provide personal development and risk-taking opportunities; and
- ◆ Construct a Transformation Plan that visibly represents the plan on a surface that is large enough for group members to gather around and write on, as seen in Figure 12.

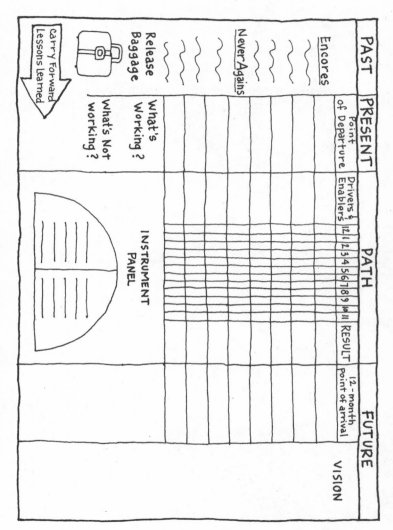

Figure 12: The Transformation Plan

It was Friday morning and we were sitting in chairs that formed a circle. Sixteen of us had been in this room since Monday, often until late into the night. Truly the most emotionally intense thing I'd ever experienced. But I'd signed on, been given the opportunity to opt out, and had chosen to go for it.

By the time Friday rolled around, I was feeling totally exposed...like all my secrets were out in the open, the best and the worst parts of me lying there in a tangled heap for all to see. But I just didn't care anymore. Others' impressions of me no longer seemed important.

I hadn't slept or eaten much all week. Hadn't wanted to. Hadn't needed to.

So there I was that morning, sitting in my chair, feeling empty and clean.

At once, a strange and wonderful energy filled my whole being. Soon my body couldn't contain it...it was as if an internal dam had broken and my spirit was pouring forth, washing across the whole universe. I felt the stream of my spirit merge with a mighty river, into which flows the spirit of every living thing, not separate and distinct, just one infinitely powerful, perfect force.

I was totally submerged in that river for about four days - washed ashore on the following Tuesday, if I recall.

Hey, if you were sitting around the circle that Friday morning, now you know what was going on with me. What about you? Did you feel it too?

CHANGE MECHANISM

We use an approach adapted from work by Sink and Morris (1995), for managing large-scale improvement in a dynamic organizational environment. It involves learning from and building on past successes and failures to move toward a future vision. It is a comprehensive and integrated strategy, which can evolve into world class transformation. This change mechanism contains four basic components:

(1) Past and Present
(2) Future
(3) Fronts
(4) Plan of Action

Past and Present

The first step is to reflect and engage in a dialogue about past and present performance initiatives. This analysis provides the baseline to learn from and build on past successes and to plan for the future.

Future

The future component compels you to imagine and articulate the results you want to create and the kind of organization you want. This change mechanism addresses vision as well as mission, purpose, operating principles, plans, strategies, and tactics of organizational subsystems know as fronts.

Fronts

Nine organizational subsystems, or fronts, need to be led, managed, and improved to accomplish the transformation. The term "front" conjures up a war metaphor. As in battle, charging ahead leaves the left and right front exposed. The secret to a successful transformation is alignment, coordination, synergy, matched progress, and balance. The fronts are:

1. **Planning** - all strategic planning systems: strategic, performance improvement, business, marketing, operations, and daily planning...the entire plan-do-study-act cycle.

2. **Measurement** - the system for sharing multiple levels of performance, including the systematic identification of information to support performance improvement.

3. **Culture** - the organization's shared values, beliefs, norms, and system to create the desired culture.

4. **Motivation**- the organizational system including inducements, recognition, and rewards.

5. **Education, Training, and Development** - the system of teaching knowledge and skills to everyone in the organization so they can personally and professionally improve.

6. **Infrastructure** - the system or internal structure by which the organization conducts business including organizational charts, position descriptions, functional responsibilities and informal relationships.

7. **Technology** - the system for managing "how we accomplish things," including methods, procedures, protocol, hardware and software, and tools.

8. **Politics** - the informal aspects of performance management

including the proactive management of key stakeholders' needs and expectations; anticipation of criticism; boundary spanning; internal communication; and working power bases.

9. **Communication** - the system of sharing information among groups and individuals to facilitate coordination, understanding, and cooperation.

Plan of Action

The final component is a detailed project plan of action and milestones, with accountable individuals to facilitate performance improvement initiatives across the fronts. The project plan of action is a scheduling and sequencing tool that monitors the balance of activities among the fronts. The plan of action is also a resource allocation tool and documents what was done when, where, and by whom to improve performance.

Implementation and deployment of strategic plans have often fallen short of expectations, which prompted Mintzberg to write *The Rise and Fall of Strategic Planning*. His message was not to quit planning but to re-engineer how organizations plan. Planning must be deployed and linked to actions and measures. In other words, strategic planning must itself be managed.

In *Built to Last*, Collins and Porras remind us of another myth about strategic planning that highly successful companies make their best moves by brilliant and complex strategic planning. Visionary companies make many breakthroughs by experimentation, trial and error, opportunism, and sometimes by accident. What looks like brilliant foresight and preplanning was often the result of "Let's try a lot of stuff and keep what works." The key lesson: Do not put blind faith in any strategic planning methodology (always do sanity checks) and do not lose the sense of serendipity and synchronicity.

Implementation Management

Following preparation of the initial transformation plan in CAMP, implementation begins. The implementation management phase converts plans to action and action to critical organizational results. The best plans are of no value if not successfully translated into action.

Success depends on maintaining focus and momentum, and on managing the implementation. A typical CAMP session outlines specific performance improvement objectives, ownership of objectives and a first cut at detailed action plans. Later additional detailed versions of the objective planning are produced.

However, the construct and format for the entire initiative has been established at CAMP and thus, fortifying the systematic change sought. Depending on the scope and nature of the performance improvement objective, the magnitude of change will vary. The needed work may entail a spectrum of efforts ranging from documenting and standardizing a key work process (systems management), to incrementally improving a work process (continuous process improvement), or achieving step-function improvement (re-engineering).

Visible Results System

Once the implementation management phase begins, the organization assesses and monitors performance against the transformation plan. Meaningful measurement is critical to the success of any transformation effort. An effective measurement system creates data, converts data into information and portrays the information in an understandable and useful fashion. Appendix F details this component.

To portray the information collected by the performance measurement system, the team creates a Visible Results System that includes a balanced scorecard portrayed in chart books and on visibility boards. This system portrays information so it can be used to make decisions and take actions.

Review Process

Establishing processes to review, monitor, and act on the knowledge gained from the Visible Results System is crucial. Without this, the Visible Results System offers little value. Review may include quarterly, one-day review sessions with the leadership team and extended system (those who attended the CAMP session), or navigation checks to evaluate the direction and speed of the transformation journey. The benefits of doing this are to determine:

- Continued validity of the transformation plan,
- Whether mid-course adjustments are needed; and
- Impact of plan implementation on organizational performance.

Advance Session

An advance or renewal session typically occurs 12-18 months after the initial CAMP. It marks the end of the first Transformation Cycle and the beginning of another. Although the objectives of this recycle session are similar to the initial CAMP, the agenda is modified to reflect experience and knowledge gained during the previous year.

"What results do we want to create for this organization?" is asked again. Some initial performance improvement objectives from the original CAMP session will have been implemented fully, others will lag behind the planned implementation, and there may be new improvement objectives.

As well, participants are invited to examine their self awareness process and the quality of their relationships. Frequently, roadblocks, baggage, and breakdowns have accumulated and festered over the past year. The advance session is an opportunity to surface and resolve what is keeping people from participating in their own transformation and that of the organization.

Ongoing Education, Training, and Development

Continuous people development is a common prescription for transformation initiatives. The Transformation Cycle emphasizes this ongoing activity. Providing the necessary knowledge and skills to teams and individuals in the transformation effort is necessary. Individuals work on personal and professional development using their Individual Development Document and targeted education/training and development activities for teams (e.g., TDT, leadership team).

Just-in-time training and development can focus on planning, measurement, project management, methods/process engineering, problem solving, decision analysis, motivation, and other areas of competence required in a transformation effort.

Although education, training and development may be offered to all organizational levels, the Leadership Team, Transformation Design Team, and implementation teams should receive more intense training since they drive the transformation.

BEYOND THE TRANSFORMATION CYCLE

The complete Transformation Cycle takes 12-18 months, depending upon the nature of the organization. The length of the cycle tends to stabilize at 12 months after the second or third cycle. Implementation management occurs during the last 7- 13 months of the cycle depending on the length of the cycle. Quarterly reviews are to look at progress and performance on the plan. At the end of the cycle, an advance/review/ renewal session is held to evaluate what worked, what did not, why, and the impact of improvement interventions on organizational performance.

At this point, the organization has begun the second cycle of transformation. The organization would not likely zero-base the plan. Instead, each year it should build, update, and enhance it. In later cycles, as the organization refines its vision, mission, and guiding principles, it should change its focus, spending more time on the visible measurement system; implementation and deployment; team building; and education, training, and development.

The organization must be serious and devote sufficient resources to the effort. If an organization does these things, it is on its way to transforming itself to a total performance organization. We believe that continuity of leadership comes in large part from the systems and the processes. Therefore, the establishment of a strong renewal system greatly benefits the organization by giving leadership a way to recreate the organization.

In my previous work at a mental health facility, I encountered Rose. Rose had been institutionalized for many years. She wouldn't communicate verbally and often became violent, toward herself and the other residents.

We had a meeting about Rose when she smashed her arm through some drywall in the house. As "experts," we each had our own ideas for addressing the situation. Because of my psychology background I recommended an extensive behavioral program. The psychiatrist in the group insisted we increase her anti-psychotic medications. Then there was Jim (name has been changed), who had just taken over as the facility's director. After listening quietly to everyone views, he offered his approach: "Physical first, then emotional, then chemical."

Rose was examined by a medical doctor, who found that screws had been put in her ankle years before to correct a bad break. Further, the doctor discovered severe calcification around the screws—an extremely painful condition. But since Rose had been non-communicative, no one had known of this affliction. Rose underwent surgery and had the screws removed. Then a miracle happened. She began using words to communicate her needs, she stopped battering herself and other patients, and, most wonderfully, she was able to come off her anti-psychotic medications.

By the time I left the home to begin my work helping organizations, Rose was a changed woman. Upon my departure, I nearly wept when she hugged me and whispered, "Goodbye and be good."

Not long into my management consulting career, I encountered a huge challenge with one organization. As I interviewed each employee, it was clear that divisions existed among both people and groups. There were even behaviors that were similar to Rose's acting out. For example, one person kept dumping their coffee in a colleague's plants to kill them.

My approach? First the physical...the management systems. The organization had resulted from a recent merger and had no clear communication lines, no decision making process, no common priorities. I worked to improve the organization's information sharing, infrastructure (roles and responsibilities), and planning systems. Indeed, we began with strategic planning to pinpoint some of the best targets for improvement. Pairing these and other systems interventions with the strong leadership has turned this organization into a vibrant community. You can see it in the people. Deming said that management's job was to remove barriers to employees' success. Once we identified and dealt with the roadblocks, the organization transformed on its own strength.

Thanks Jim. Thanks Rose.

My aunt was the wife of an itinerant minister, and for years she worked seven days a week to support him. He served several small, rural churches, and when he retired she said, "I've been waiting all these years to sit down and put my feet up."

So my aunt bought a nice big chair and sat down. For awhile she marveled at the concept of just sitting, and we who watched her sit did so with a good measure of satisfaction. But the longer she sat, the harder it became for her to get up out of the chair.

And now she sits in her chair for the most part of each day. Only her chair has wheels, her bed has rails, and her meals are spoon fed by a nurse.

Moral of the story: KEEP MOVING!

SUMMARY POINTS

- ◆ Organizational transformations include:
  - ◆ Individual reaction curves
  - ◆ Organizational reaction curves
  - ◆ Individual creation journeys
  - ◆ Organizational creation journeys

  - ◆ A transformation plan must reflect individual intentions, occur at all levels, involve a creation mindset, and include representation from the extended system.

- ◆ The components of The Transformation Cycle include:
  - ◆ Situation Appraisal
  - ◆ Formation of the Transformation Design and Leadership Teams
  - ◆ Transformation Design
  - ◆ All-Hands Information Sharing
  - ◆ CAMP Pre-Work
  - ◆ CAMP Session
  - ◆ Implementation Management
  - ◆ Visible Results System
  - ◆ Review Process
  - ◆ Advance and Renewal Session
  - ◆ Ongoing Education, Training and Development

QUESTIONS AND REFLECTIONS

Does my workplace have a sense of shared community? If so, how would I describe it? What is my level of commitment to improve my workplace community?

Does my organization have the discipline to transform itself?

Who are the architects/engineers of my organization's transformation?

Is there a blueprint for organizational change?

Am I a designer, developer, and/or agent of change? If so, how?

On a scale of 1-10, how is my organization performing with respect to managing:
Planning, Infrastructure, Learning, Communication, Culture, Motivation, Measurement, Technology, Politics.

How much do the people in my organization know about the organizational vision? How involved are they in creating it?

Do my organizational stakeholders regularly meet to set strategy and make decisions to improve my organization?

Do I understand the key result areas for my organization?

A Final Thought

IT IS HAPPENING NOW

Awaken! A fundamental change in how we conduct organizational business is occurring. Rekindle the spirit of self-creation, and join with others in the celebration of this evolutionary leap.

Work miracles are within reach for everyone. The power is yours to transform yourself and your workplace. A host of individuals within organizations are awakening to this power.

Our environment today is peppered with organizations that leverage empowered workforces to create incredible results. Perfection is not required, but clear intention to create the desired workplace is necessary. There is no doubt than gaining clear intention is challenging.

The first hurdle is formulating an answer to, "What is my purpose in life?" Tools such as the Individual Development Document can assist in structured thinking. But, the question of life's purpose is colossal. So, get started with a first version and revise it as your wisdom grows. Then, with an idea of why you are here, construct a Life Plan to serve as a blueprint to fulfill your purpose.

A collective purpose and vision must be established for the organization. New methods are emerging to do this. Unlike the old process where senior leadership brings the vision and strategic plan down from the mountaintop, new methods capture the essence and creative spirit of all within the organization.

New leadership is required to channel this creative energy. Transformational leaders must quickly build trust, coach others to define and fulfill their dreams, clearly express passion, and have a keen sense of organizational success requirements. The community vision alignment approach incorporates these leadership skills in its design while rejecting the coercive, manipulative and at best, parental approach of old.

Since the transformation journey is perplexing, a roadmap is essential. The Transformation Cycle is but one roadmap that can guide you to a new organization. It has been effective in many workplaces.

Your intention to create an enlivened workplace will lead you to the right tools. Many outstanding tools abound. Intention to use these tools with clarity of purpose is the valuable ingredient.

Organizations continue to differentiate themselves as problem-solving versus creation entities. Outcomes in creation communities can appear impossible when in fact they are simply the expression of channeled human spirit. To channel spiritual energy within your organization, you must:

- simplify your approach to organizational change and transformation;
- focus on helping yourself and others becoming crystal clear on the business results you want to create;
- acknowledge that all the answers needed to move you and your organization towards the desired state are within reach; and
- accept that the tools and techniques to enable success are available if your intention is clear.

How can you help yourself and those in your organization undertake this challenge? We have found that clear intention starts with looking in the mirror at yourself, your relationships, and what you want to create. Realized intention (your desired result) is the surprisingly natural outcome of this introspection.

In order to help people clarify intention, create results, and take ownership of the organization, you must see them as extensions of yourself. People need care, understanding, freedom, development, and growth opportunities. You must at the same time see people as separate entities with their own visions and aspirations, with paths that may or may not be completely aligned with the vision of the organization.

Since opportunity resides in creation, spirited organizations will grow while traditional organizations will fail. As individuals develop higher levels of consciousness, they create and strengthen conscious organizations. Self-aware, spirit-filled individuals are drawn to these successful and empowering organizations, thus, intensifying their evolution. Those who hold on to buggy whip organizations of the past will mourn their extinction.

On a larger scale, we firmly believe that an age of collective awareness is upon us. We have seen the power of collective, purposeful action in the past. Now we are witnessing enormous growth in our abilities to use collective consciousness to seize the complex opportunities arising today.

APPENDICES

A.   Life Plan

B.   Situation Appraisal

C.   Team Charter Elements

D.   About CAMP: Creating Alignment to Maximize Performance

E.   Letters From CAMP

F.   Visible Results System

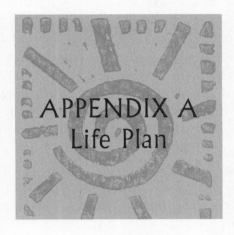

APPENDIX A
Life Plan

What is a Life Plan?
The Life Plan is both a document and process, which connects our daily activities with our deeper understanding of what gives meaning to our lives. Creating a Life Plan helps us define our personal goals and aspirations: what we want to create of ourselves and in the world around us.

Why Create a Life Plan?
There is a great deal of power in having both a personal vision and a clear picture of our current reality. Having this perspective will generate a force within us, which will move us toward our vision, and the production of tangible results.

Wherever You Are, Start There.
It has been our experience that people often hesitate to take the first step in developing a Life Plan. One reason is that many people believe that the document must be perfect and complete. Quite the opposite is intended. The Life Plan is a life long working document. Begin with an imperfect first version knowing that you will enhance it over time. The key is to start.

Re-Visiting the Life Plan.
The Life Plan is intended to be a living document. We suggest you revisit your Life Plan once every year, and perhaps more frequently in times of rapid personal change. Many people prefer to re-examine their Life Plan near their birthdays.

SIGNIFICANT LIFE EVENTS
A significant life event is a specific happening...a critical incident...a key episode in your past, set in a particular time and place. It is a specific moment in your life that stands out to you for some reason. Describe several of the most critical incidents in your life to date. What was the impact of these events on the course of your life and who you are as a person?

JOY
What gives you joy? Under what circumstances do you experience the feeling of joy?

VALUES & PRINCIPLES
Core values need no rational or external justification, nor do they sway with trends and fads of the day. Principles are self-evident guidelines for human conduct, basic truths.

What are your personal core values? Which principles are most important to you? What values and principles do you live by?

LIFE PURPOSE
What is your purpose for being?

5-YEAR IMAGE
When you fast-forward your life's videotape five years ahead, what do you see? Who are you and how are you engaged in life?

PLANNING THE PARTS OF THE WHOLE
In this section, seven areas of life are offered. However, other areas can be added or substituted in order to better fit your mental breakdown of your life's major areas. Within each area, you are asked to describe a future vision (or point of arrival), a current state (or point of departure), and the actions required to achieve your vision. For each area in which you want to focus, establish one or more specific, measurable goals and outline your current performance related to these goals.

As you complete this section, don't feel pressured to sign up for aggressive goals in each area. While it can be appealing and seductive to set aggressive goals, try to focus on what is realistic for you. Most of us have experienced disappointment in the area of goal setting – unmet New Year's resolutions are a common example. Our suggestion is to focus your goals on three to five areas. Consider the option of merely maintaining and monitoring other areas in which you've chosen not to focus.

If you're struggling with which projects to take on, please stop for a minute, and review your work in earlier sections.

Re-read your life's purpose, your principles, your values, etc. Trust these core areas to guide you in this planning process.

SPIRITUAL

Point of Arrival (result you choose to create on the spiritual horizon):

Point of Departure (results you are currently creating on the spiritual horizon):

Actions Required/Milestones:

1.   Specific Measurable Goals:

Current Results:

2.   Specific Measurable Goals:

Current Results:

3.   Specific Measurable Goals:

Current Results:

FAMILY

Point of Arrival (result you choose to create on the family horizon):

Point of Departure (results you are currently creating on the family horizon):

Actions Required/Milestones:

1. Specific Measurable Goals:

    Current Results:

2. Specific Measurable Goals:

    Current Results:

3. Specific Measurable Goals:

    Current Results:

INTELLECTUAL GROWTH

Point of Arrival (result you choose to create on the intellectual growth horizon):

Point of Departure (results you are currently creating on the intellectual growth horizon):

Actions Required/Milestones:

1.   Specific Measurable Goals:

Current Results:

2.   Specific Measurable Goals:

Current Results:

3.   Specific Measurable Goals:

Current Results:

PHYSICAL

Point of Arrival (result you choose to create on the physical horizon):

Point of Departure (results you are currently creating on the physical horizon):

Actions Required/Milestones:

1.   Specific Measurable Goals:
Current Results:

2.   Specific Measurable Goals:

Current Results:

3.   Specific Measurable Goals:

Current Results:

VOCATIONAL

Point of Arrival (result you choose to create on the vocational horizon):

Point of Departure (results you are currently creating on the vocational horizon):

Actions Required/Milestones:

1.   Specific Measurable Goals:

Current Results:

2.   Specific Measurable Goals:

Current Results:

3.   Specific Measurable Goals:

Current Results:

FINANCIAL

Point of Arrival (result you choose to create on the financial horizon):

Point of Departure (results you are currently creating on the financial horizon):

Actions Required/Milestones:

1. Specific Measurable Goals:

   Current Results:

2. Specific Measurable Goals:

   Current Results:

3. Specific Measurable Goals:

   Current Results:

COMMUNITY

Point of Arrival (result you choose to create on the community horizon):

Point of Departure (results you are currently creating on the community horizon):

Actions Required/Milestones:

1.   Specific Measurable Goals:

Current Results:

2.   Specific Measurable Goals:

Current Results:

3.   Specific Measurable Goals:

Current Results:

CONDITIONS FOR SUCCESS

What are the conditions, internal to you, that you need in order to succeed in the areas you have declared (e.g., state of mind, state of being, approaches to life, personal skills.)? What are the conditions external to you, that you need in order to succeed (e.g., family, support)?

APPENDIX B
Situation Appraisal

OBJECTIVE

This is a tool to determine the current state of an organization for the purpose of future improvement. Thirteen areas are investigated and provide the information required to build a comprehensive improvement plan. Creating the organization desired requires knowledge of current state, where the organization is presently.

1 = Strongly Disagree; 2 = Disagree; 3 = Neutral;
4 = Agree; 5 = Strongly Agree

PLANNING

Clear, comprehensive system for strategic, tactical, operational, and improvement planning exists.

1   2   3   4   5

Planning system involves the extended system (Customers, suppliers, up-line, down-line).

1   2   3   4   5

Planning system focuses on both long and short term goals and objectives.

1   2   3   4   5

Strategic, tactical, operational, and improvement planning are well integrated.

1   2   3   4   5

Systematic review and improvement of the planning system is in place and effective.

1   2   3   4   5

Describe your planning system (strategic, tactical, operational, and improvement).

Who is involved in the planning process (customers, stakeholders, suppliers, up-line, down-line)? How are they involved?

How are your 15, 10, 5 year goals incorporated? What is the organization's time frame for planning?

How are systems (strategic, tactical, improvement) linked? What does the flow of information between the systems look like? Who is involved in each type? Are those responsible for implementing the plans involved in developing the plan?

How effective is your current planning system? How do you know? What is the PDSA cycle associated with planning?

INFRASTRUCTURE

Organizational structure supports the short and long term goals and objectives of the organization.

1   2   3   4   5

Visible, clear linkage between organizational objectives, team actions, and individual work plans.

1   2   3   4   5

Describe your organizational structure. What is your structure for doing your work? For handling crises? For improvement? How do these structures support the organization's goals?

Describe your work. How does it relate to the organization's goals? How do the teams you are on relate to organizational goals?

How do you (your team) make decisions? How much authority do you (your team) have? Responsibility?

What is your process for starting up teams? Are there team charters? What do the charters involve? Team training? Clear purpose?

MEASUREMENT

Visible measurement system is in place, reflecting both process and results measures.

1   2   3   4   5

Systematic and ongoing efforts to improve the measurement system.

1   2   3   4   5

Clear line of sight measures exist from the individual to the organization.

1   2   3   4   5

Meaningful benchmarking is performed.

1   2   3   4   5

Describe your measurement system. Are the measures visible? Examples of process and result measures. How is the information used? To make what types of decisions?

How do you apply PDSA to your measurement system? Who is responsible for improving the measurement system? What improvements are being made to what and how you measure?

How do your measures link to the organization's measures? What impact does improving your area have on the whole organization? How do you know?

Do your measures cover financials? Internal business processes? Employee measures? Customer satisfaction? Innovation?

Do you benchmark? Within industry? Outside industry? What lessons have you learned through benchmarking within the last 2 years?

EDUCATION, TRAINING, AND DEVELOPMENT

Clear, communicated ET&D plans in place to support the organization's objectives.

1   2   3   4   5

Individuals improving both professionally and personally.

1   2   3   4   5

ET&D is driven by a customer focus.

1   2   3   4   5

Systematic review and improvement performed on the ET&D system.

1   2   3   4   5

Involvement of a cross-section of employees in developing and owning the ET&D plan.

1   2   3   4   5

Describe your ET&D system. How does ET&D support organizational objectives? Does everyone in the organization know what the ET&D plan is?

Is your ET&D system providing a balance of professional and personal development for individuals?

How do you determine ET&D needs? How do you determine ET&D expectations? How do you determine the skill level of the work force?

How do you determine the effectiveness of the ET&D system?

How do you develop internal resources to continue the training? Is your training based on skills? Knowledge? Do you have clearly defined outcomes and outputs for training? Who develops the ET&D plan? How are employees involved in the development?

MOTIVATION

Effective performance management system in place and understood by all employees.

1   2   3   4   5

Employees experience the meaningfulness in their work.

1   2   3   4   5

Clearly defined measures for the motivation system exist.

1   2   3   4   5

Employees have the knowledge of the results their actions produce.

1   2   3   4   5

Full complement of strategies to initiate, direct, and sustain desired individual and team behavior.

1   2   3   4   5

Describe your performance management system. How is this system communicated to employees? How do you determine if the system is effective?

How do you view your work? What is its purpose? Why do you show up each day? What are your rewards for a job well done?

Does the organization recognize the individual contribution of its members? If so, how?

How do you know if your rewards and recognition system is effective? What measures are in place to determine motivation level? Do you have the knowledge of the results you produce? What is the link between your actions and organizational results?

Do you have defined desired individual behaviors? Team behaviors? What different methods do you use to develop those behaviors? What is the role of intrinsic/extrinsic rewards?

COMMUNICATION

Diversity of effective information sharing approaches.
1   2   3   4   5

Communication is open, honest, direct.
1   2   3   4   5

Organizational values/operating principles and vision are communicated and reinforced by action.
1   2   3   4   5

Employees share individual responsibility shared to be informed.
1   2   3   4   5

Formal feedback loop between employees and management is established and used.
1   2   3   4   5

Describe your communication system. What methods do you use to communicate? What information is shared using each method? How is effectiveness determined? Understanding / Change in attitudes / Change in behavior?

What affect do you have for organizational communication? Is communication open, honest, direct? Does communication stimulate trust?

What organizational information is shared with employees? What are the organization's values / operating principles? What is the organization's vision? How are they communicated? Reinforced by action?

Do employees share the responsibility to remain informed?

How do employees and management communicate? What feed-back loops are used? How are supervisors incorporated into the communication process?

TECHNOLOGY

Continuous improvement process is standardized and utilized throughout the organization.

1   2   3   4   5

Core business processes are defined, mapped, and well-documented.

1   2   3   4   5

Use of leading edge technology in core work.

1   2   3   4   5

Problem solving process is standardized and utilized throughout the organization.

1   2   3   4   5

Use of data/information in decision making is pervasive.

1   2   3   4   5

Do you use the methods / techniques / tools for continuous process improvement? How? How are learnings from using these tools shared within the organization?

What are your core business processes? Have they been defined thoroughly? Are they well documented?

How do you stay on the cutting edge of your core business technology? What have been recent improvements in how you do your work?

What processes do you use to solve problems? How are learnings shared? Do you reward innovation and creativity in improvement efforts? How?

How do you make decisions? What information are you not currently getting that you need?

POLITICS

Commitment for change is managed effectively with all stakeholders.
1   2   3   4   5

All significant stakeholders in change are known and involved in the change effort.
1   2   3   4   5

Key people with informal and formal power are aligned with the organization's direction.
1   2   3   4   5

Critics are involved in the change effort.
1   2   3   4   5

Bases of power (both formal and informal) are known and managed.
1   2   3   4   5

Who are the key stakeholders in your change effort? Internal? External? Up-line? Down-line? Suppliers? Customers?

How do you keep the key stakeholders involved and committed to the change effort?

What are the key bases of power in the organization? Management? Workers? Informal? Formal? How do you manage their alignment to the organization's direction?

How do you handle critics? How do you incorporate them into the change effort?

How do manage power in the organization? What knowledge is shared about the bases of power?

CULTURE

Trust level among key personnel is improving.

1   2   3   4   5

Values and operating principles have been developed and communicated.

1   2   3   4   5

Decisions are made in the context of values and operating principles.

1   2   3   4   5

Employees demonstrate a personal ownership for the organization.

1   2   3   4   5

Employees demonstrate a personal ownership
for the organization.

1   2   3   4   5

A conscious effort is underway to shape the culture to support change.

1   2   3   4   5

What is the level of trust within the organization? How do you know? What steps are being taken to improve the level of trust between key players in the change effort?

How are the organization's values reinforced by action? How do employees align with the values?

Are organizational values incorporated in the decision making process? Is the organization's vision and goals within the context of the organization's values?

How do employees feel about the organization? How do they demonstrate ownership for the organization?

What is the process for influencing organizational culture? How willing is the organization to change?

LEADERSHIP

Autonomy is pervasive and leadership is shared.
1   2   3   4   5

Leadership demonstrates openness to different points of view and new ideas.
1   2   3   4   5

Leadership holds people accountable for achieving results.
1   2   3   4   5

Leadership celebrates success and new learnings, including learning from errors in the past.
1   2   3   4   5

Leadership provides organization with the tools and resources needed to achieve objectives.
1   2   3   4   5

Describe the leadership of this organization. How much autonomy do you see at your level? How is leadership shared?

How does leadership model the organization's values and operating principles? How does leadership react to alternative points of view? What new ideas have been implemented recently?

Does leadership hold people accountable for results? In what ways? How is this responsibility shared within teams?

What new learnings has the organization had recently? How were these learnings shared? Give an example of celebrating the successes and learnings from the past.

How has organizational leadership provided tools to achieve objectives? What interactions do leaders have? What tools are you lacking to achieve the vision?

BURNING PLATFORM

Clearly defined and communicated need to change.
1   2   3   4   5

Employees recognize the importance of the change effort.
1   2   3   4   5

Environment has been scanned and analyzed for the future requirements for work.
1   2   3   4   5

Clear understanding of what the "best in class" are doing.
1   2   3   4   5

Professional change is seen as necessary and important.
1   2   3   4   5

Describe your organization's mandate for change. Why does your organization need to change? How is this message communicated throughout the organization?
How do employees react to the message of change?

What are the environmental factors involved in the change? What are the future requirements of your work?

What does "best in class" mean for your industry? Who is a model for the future? In what ways?

How do individuals view the need to change? In what ways will the individual benefit? What is the cost? How must you change within your profession?

CREATION / VISION

Clearly defined, consensus-generated vision of the organization.
1   2   3   4   5

Vision is communicated throughout the organization on an on-going basis.
1   2   3   4   5

Consistent demonstration of leadership's personal connection to the vision.
1   2   3   4   5

Consistent demonstration of personal vision alignment with organizational vision.
1   2   3   4   5

Tactical and operational objectives are in place to support the vision.
1   2   3   4   5

What is the organization's vision? How was it developed?

How has the vision been communicated to all employees? What are the plans to communicate the vision?

How does leadership demonstrate its connection to the vision? What behaviors do the leaders demonstrate?

How do individuals demonstrate their personal vision? How do these align with the organization's vision?

What tactical objectives do you have? How will these support achieving the vision? What operational objectives are in place?

PAST

Past learnings are captured and analyzed.
1   2   3   4   5
Consistent record of the past.
1   2   3   4   5
Organization does not live in the past.
1   2   3   4   5

Past is celebrated.
1   2   3   4   5
Past is not a barrier to change.
1   2   3   4   5

How is the past recorded? What have you learned from the organization's past? What would the organization repeat? What would the organization not do again?

Where is the record of the past kept? Is it consistent over time?

How is the past celebrated? In what ways? Successes and failures?

APPENDIX C
Team Charter Elements

Mission

Provides direction to the team. Why does this team exist? What specific results or objectives must be accomplished as part of the mission?

Sponsor

Provides accountability and guidance to the team. Who is the chartering individual or group? To whom is the team accountable for results? What is the reporting frequency to the sponsor?

Boundaries

Defines the scope of work for the team. What part of the organization (or product or process) will the team focus on? What constraints or limits must the team work within? At what point does the team's work end?

Authority and Decision Rules

Defines who has decision authority over which issues. What decisions can the team make on its own and not tell anyone? What decisions must the team inform others of once the decision is made? What decisions must the team seek permission from the sponsor for?

Membership

Defines who is on the team and where they come from, who they represent. What skills and viewpoints are needed on the team? Who are the permanent members? Who are the ad-hoc or temporary members? Who has decision authority to add or drop members?

Roles & Responsibilities

Clarifies roles within the team. What formal roles (team leader, convener, facilitator, recorder, logistics, etc.) will the team use to distribute workload? What are the specific responsibilities of each member?

Products

Defines what deliverables the team is expected to produce. What plans, reports, documents, etc. does the sponsor expect the team to create?

Customers

Defines who receives the products of the team. Which individuals or groups does the team provide specific products or services to?

Key Inputs

Defines what deliverables the team expects to receive from its suppliers. What plans, reports, documents, etc. does the team require from its suppliers?

Key Suppliers

Defines people, not on the team, who provide inputs to the team. From which individuals or groups does the team receive products or services?

Timeline

Defines time constraints for the team. What are the key milestones for mission accomplishment?

Measures of Effectiveness

Defines success for the team. What are the key measures of effectiveness that will be used to define success? Who will assess the performance of the team and when?

Team to Team Interactions

Defines interactions and communications with other teams. With what other groups and teams must this team interact and coordinate? In what ways and how often will the team coordinate and communicate with these other groups and teams?

Resources to the Team

Defines the resources the team has available. What resources can the team call upon?

Intrateam Processes

Defines how the team will function. How often and where will the team meet? How will the team make decisions in a group setting? What principles will be used in making decisions?

Ground Rules

Define how team members will behave toward one another. What rules does the team want to live by?

Team Self-Assessment

Defines improvement processes for the team. How and when will the team assess its own processes and progress and performance? When and how will the team review and update the charter?

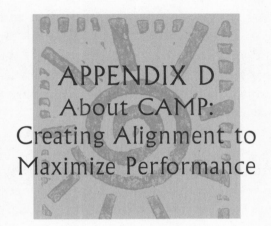

APPENDIX D
About CAMP:
Creating Alignment to
Maximize Performance

CAMP facilitates the development of creation communities and increases individual intention within these communities. This intervention couples the power of group and individual intention with a strong planning mechanism. This part of the Transformation Cycle, explained in Chapter 5, can be used with other interventions to produce dramatic, long-term results.

CAMP is a five-day, off-site attended by 10-50 people from a specific business unit. In addition, extended system representatives such as customers and suppliers may attend.

The purpose of CAMP is to develop a mechanism for organizational growth, such as a strategic plan and/or visible results system. Equally important, CAMP develops individual intention and organizational community. CAMP is usually undertaken near the beginning of a transformation effort to create the personal and group conditions that ensure the success of the improvement effort.

In every CAMP, people have experienced profound change. Some sessions involve growing personally, building trust, listening actively, using feedback, or shifting paradigms. Since CAMP involves both a change mechanism and a focus on mental stances, proper sequencing and timing are necessary to ensure effectiveness.

Implementing an organizational change process without addressing personal issues is problematic. Therefore, it is most effective to start with intention. On the first day, we focus exclusively on intention and over the next four days gradually focus on the transformation mechanism. By the fifth day, mechanism comprises the majority of our time. Intention has become part of the culture of the group and is visible in all participants.

The Social Psychology of CAMP

Let's look at a typical CAMP session. At the beginning of the first day, the group feels pretty good. Our CAMP group starts with pseudocommunity, the period of pretending that community already exists. Often, there's denial of conflict, pain, and differences among members. There is a strong sense of politeness and harmony usually to the point of insincerity and dishonesty. Early in the session, hurt feelings are ignored or denied, and open conflict is avoided.

As CAMP progresses on the first day, individual differences inevitably emerge as people express more authenticity. As these differences become apparent, the group may enter the chaos stage, characterized by attempts to eliminate differences among members.

As the group progresses beyond chaos, it enters the emptiness stage and rids itself of everything that prevents the community formation. This can include personal issues such as anger and grief. Individuals in this stage often risk disclosing hidden negative feelings to the group. The group may have feelings of relief, but also opposing feelings comparable to dying.

After emptying, the group may shift dramatically into the community phase. Now individuals truly communicate; they both speak sincerely and hear accurately. Individuals tend to experience a sense of inner peace and group harmony. During this stage, there is so much cooperation that participants describe it as a peak experience.

The first step to make a group more self-aware occurs during kickoff in the pseudocommunity phase. Individual, one-on-one, and group catharses help participants open themselves to the possibilities of what they can create together. Since CAMP results in the examination of personal issues and the struggle with baggage, the facilitator needs to be supportive and be able to handle extreme emotional displays.

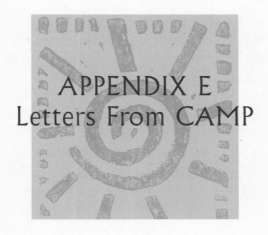

APPENDIX E
Letters From CAMP

These letters were written by CAMP participants. These letters reflect the thoughts, feelings, insights, heartaches, breakthroughs, joy, curiosities, and mysteries we've experienced in the growth and development of creation communities as we approach the new millenium.

We hope you enjoy and are inspired by them.

Dear Source,

I can't believe it is starting to make sense. The models presented during CAMP were tough to digest. As the leader encouraged us to try on "a new coat" of ideas, I found it difficult to listen to what seemed like academic models before shouting the idea would not work. Some of the concepts seemed to make sense, but others appeared to be counter-intuitive.

We were encouraged to be open to the concept of 1 percent possibility of being right, just the slightest chance that something had a kernel of truth. I don't mind telling you this was tough! I was tempted to dismiss or alter each concept to my own current thinking. I could see how closed I was to new ideas.

And what if the concept was on the mark? What would it mean to my beliefs on which I had built my current house of ideas? I did notice my tendency to avoid accepting a possibility for even a nano-second. For some reason, some ideas threatened my way of thinking.

The funny thing was that during the night, the ideas I avoided the most crept into my thoughts. They worked on me. I wrestled with their meaning and application to my world.

Toying with the possibility there was some truth hidden in the abstractions, I noticed that slowly my world began to change. Not at a fast rate, mind you. But I began to see new things encompassed in old actions. Some past obstacles and problems appeared different and invited more understanding. I was able to see and understand my connection to the events around me For example, take how my life has developed. Yes, I know that much of my life was driven by my actions or inactions, but certainly not all of the results. At least I did not think so.

As I took a look at the good things I have accomplished in my life, some connections become clear. My college education and the hard work I put into my career created my successes. The estranged relationship with my older sister was not my fault; it was the way she wanted it to be. Even when I was thinking this exception to the principle of connectiveness (at cause), the trainer's words came back to be the difference between being connected versus being at fault. Yes, my sister and I had made many choices in our relationship that led us to this point.

Often I would chalk up my actions as reactions to her stubbornness or meanness, but the reactions were my choice too. I could even see how the actions I took deepened our rift when we were teenagers eventually leading to a distant relationship in our adulthood.

I can see that the actions I took contributed to the current state with my sister. However, more importantly the ability to make change appears to be obvious. As the trainer said, the opportunity to create what we want in our lives is present with us every moment…in the present as well as in the future. Learnings from the past can be helpful and planning for the future is wise, but the power is in the present to form the life we desire and the relationships that we hunger for.

Dear God,

All I can do is think! I'm sure these people are people. That's about all I'm sure of ... and I'm sure I'm a person.

Now, to break that paradigm. I don't know what we are!? In any case, I believe we can be conscious of being light and share our learnings with others on the planet.

Sometimes my head really hurts from all this. I feel like a lion in my chest......strong of heart. My head is not always clear. When my head is clear, I think of how to move things along.

Move these people. Move myself... go to another level of awareness. Move!

I keep thinking about what John (the facilitator) said last night. "There's nothing to get. When you're hot you're hot, when you're not you're not." Maybe that's it.

Dear Universe,

After observing during this morning's session, I decided to take a risk. This is powerful — open, honest, direct communication in front of my boss and the leadership team. But if they're committed like I am to this organization, they need to know. I was concerned that what I said would come back to haunt me.

Having done the trust exercise, though, I feel much better about this new way of approaching business (life!). What's left for me to do is to strive to be self-aware in life and at work.

Wait! Is striving like trying? I need 100 percent intention to drive this task. I'm about self-improvement; I need to back my learning with motivation/intention. I'm excited about what's possible with my new approach, though I'm not sure it's going to be easy dealing with the honest introspection to make this journey. One thing's for sure, this isn't going to be the usual comfortable do-nothing. I'm getting things done!

Dear _____,

   I understand that your team is about to participate in a CAMP. How exciting! Just wanted to drop you a note encouraging you to take the risk in getting the extended system (key customers, board members, suppliers and line personnel) to attend.

   As you know, my small manufacturing company held a CAMP last summer. I was real hesitant to throw myself and key leaders, let alone my key customers and stakeholders, into this event. The first couple of days were real tense as all of us were taken through some exercises that revealed our true intentions. I was concerned about my customers seeing the warts of our operation. However, I must say that the experience brought the whole body of participants, all individuals close together.

   There is something about getting honest about your individual and collective strengths, growth opportunities, and current results that is freeing. Our strategic plan that we produced during the latter part of the week reflected this honesty and creative spirit. Differing from or previous plans, I know that the action plans behind our strategic choices will be achieved this time. As an extended system, we saw clearly where our creative energies exist and what we intend to accomplishment.

   We have been marching toward our future ever since. I trust you will throw yourself to this great opportunity. We'll talk after you have experienced CAMP.

APPENDIX F
Visible Results System

The Visible Results System (VRS) is an approach developed by The Performance Center for installing performance metrics within an organization. The intervention approach is based upon theory from: strategic management, goal-setting, large-group interventions, and self-efficacy. The visible measurement system is designed and applied such that it:

◆ links corporate objectives with lower level tactics and activities for performance improvement;
◆ focuses the organization on the organization's priority areas;
◆ supports the application of data-analysis techniques, process management and total quality management;
◆ provides a systematic process for reviewing and understanding results, and initiating timely countermeasures; and

+ provides participants with the skills (tools and techniques) and understanding (motivation) to be accountable for achieving performance targets.

Method of Intervention

The approach is based upon a demonstrated intervention philosophy. This philosophy is founded in the belief that interventions are most effective when seen as a business requirement and as integrated with existing work. The intervention is divided into steps that are delivered as workshops.

+ Step One: Organizational System Analysis – Following the establishment of corporate objectives and strategies during strategic planning, the appropriate next level of the organization is updated. Getting others with responsibility for performance improvement on the same 'sheet' in terms of direction and the basis for the direction is a very important step in the improvement process. The update includes the following: the corporate vision, the near-term direction of the corporation, significant changes on the horizon, customer satisfaction, competitive position, the current levels of performance, and the required levels of performance. During the one-day workshop, the target organization begins to build their 'planning wall.'

+ Step Two: Performance Improvement Techniques – During the second workshop, the organization gains knowledge and skills about performance improvement techniques. Our approach to performance management differs from management by objectives (MBO). With MBO, individuals are given targets and expected to achieve the targets. The improvement process is rarely specified. Our approach is consistent with Total Quality Management. Individuals not only are expected to achieve targets, but they are also expected to improve processes. Long–term sustainable results are achieved through process improvement. Process improvement requires the ability to collect and analyze data and then use the information to make decisions regarding action.

In between the workshops, we assist individuals as they apply the tools and techniques within their areas of responsibility. During the workshops, participants work with their own data (when they have it). Depending upon the existing level of knowledge, a series of workshops can be designed which provided individuals or teams with tools and techniques for improving process performance.

The workshops are tailored to the specific needs and strategy of the organization. The workshops are designed to address specific technical needs or present a more general approach to problem solving and performance improvement. The workshops are divided into 'bite-size' pieces so that participants are exposed to concepts and definitions, practice an example or two and then are asked to apply the techniques towards their improvement are a prior to the next workshop. At the workshops, individuals share their learnings in application and their progress in creating improvement plans. Each application exercise moves individuals or teams forward in formulating and implementing their performance improvement plan. An example of a process management ciriculum is provided below.

A. Data Analysis I: *Process Management* – the use of flow charts to analyze work processes, the identification of result and process indicators.
B. Data Analysis II: *Working with Numbers part 1* – pareto charts, histograms, multi-criteria decision making.
C. Data Analysis III: *Working with Numbers part 2* – run charts and statistical process control.
D. Data Analysis IV: *Project Management* – performance improvement plans, flagcharts, gap analysis.

• <u>Step Three: Creating Alignment to Maximize Performance (CAMP)</u> – Even with well-defined improvement plans, we have seen many organizations not achieve long term, sustainable results. Often individual and/or team attitudes and behaviors become barriers to change. During CAMP, participants gain an appreciation that any change in their professional or personal life begins with an individual choosing to make a difference in the role they have played in the past and will play in the future in improving organizational performance. At the conclusion of the session, participants declare what they can be counted on in terms of their commitments and areas of responsibility.

• <u>Step Four: Performance Reviews</u> – Establishing a method to regularly review performance status is critical. The purpose of the review process is to systematically study whether the improvement plans are being executed effectively and are achieving expected results. Implementation effectiveness is higher when regular review sessions are held. Regular review sessions establish that the work is important and create a regular forum for senior management and the improvement team to share lessons learned. Regular reviews also increase individual accountability and urgency for delivering results.

Reviews are held monthly. After several months, a mid-year review is designed as a one-day revisit to CAMP (or MINI-CAMP). After individuals are operating within the new measurement t system for a few months, barriers are more apparent than at the beginning of the intervention. A return to the CAMP environment refocused energy on the desired improvements versus the barriers to the improvements. Several months following the MINI-CAMP the first quarterly review occurs. In a quarterly review, the linkage between activities and the overall objective are studied to determine whether a relationship exists and if so, how strong a relationship.

General Learnings about Executing The Intervention
* Timing the intervention to coincide with the normal business planning cycle integrates the intervention with on-going work vs. having the intervention becoming additional work.
* The monthly reviews between managers and their management increases accountability. The reviews also provide a forum for performance discussions.
* The tools and techniques force data-based decision-making.
* The intervention aids the executive in understanding where

the real issues are in performance improvement (people, process, or equipment).

* The intervention must be visibly led by the site's ranking executive. Industrial engineering effort is required to support data collection. Quality specialists are required to support process management techniques.

* An Events Planning Team is necessary to plan and coordinate the logistics for the workshops, which comprise the intervention.

* Process management skills are a pre-requisite skill in the VRS intervention process. If the majority of the participants do not have process management training, the 3 day training should be delivered as Workshop 2. If the majority of the participants have had process management training then Workshop 2 is used to: 1)re-familiarize the group with process management tools and techniques; 2) show how process management and the VRS Intervention are complementary; and 3)utilize the quality specialists in the VRS Intervention. NOTE: Workshop 2 is led by the organization's quality specialists.

REFERENCES

Adams, Scott (1996). *The Dilbert Principle*. New York: Harper Business.

Barel, Gary (1997). "What Have We Learned About Trust From Recent Experiences with Teaming and Empowerment?" Business & Professional Ethics Journal, spring, vol 16, no. 1-3, p. 205.

Barker, J. A. (1990). *The Power of Vision: Discovering the Future*. Charthouse Learning Corporation.

Barker, Joel A. (1993). *Paradigms: The Business of Discovering the Future*. New York: HarperBusiness.

Bennis, Warren (1989). *On Becoming A Leader*. New York: Addison Wesley.

Bennis, Warren (1992) *On Becoming a Leader*. Massachusetts, Addison-Wesley Publishing Company.

Bennis, Warren (1993). *An Invented Life: Reflections on Leadership and Change*. Reading, Massachusetts, Addison-Wesley Publishing Company.

Bigley, Gregory A. and Pearce, Jone L. (1998). "Straining for Shared Meaning in Organization Science: Problems of Trust and Distrust." The Academy of Management Review, July, vol. 23, no. 3, p405-421.

Black, Kurt. (1993). *The Performance Center Position Paper Series #37: Hoshin Kanri*. Virginia Tech.

Blau, Peter (1964). *Exchange and Power in Social Life*. New York: Wiley.

Bunker, Barbara and Alban, Billie (1997). Large Group Interventions: Engaging the Whole System for Rapid Change. San Francisco, Jossey-Bass

Bunker, Barbara and Alban, Billie (1997). Large Group Interventions: Engaging the Whole System for Rapid Change. San Francisco, Jossey-Bass

Campbell, Joseph (1988). *An Open Life* in conversation with Michael Toms. Burnett, NY: Larson Publications.

Clark, Altyn and Hacker, Stephen K. (1997). Transformation Technology - An Integrated Approach. Blacksburg, Va: Insight

Chadwick-Jones, J.K. (1976). *Social Exchange Theory: its structure and influence in social psychology.* London, Academic Press.

Chopra, Deepak (1994). *The Seven Laws of Success: A Practical Guide to the Fulfillment of Your Dreams.* London: Bantam.

Chopra, Deepak (1993). *Ageless Body, Timeless Mind: The Quantum Alternative to Growing Old (1st ed.).* New York: Harmony Books.

Daley, Dennis M. and Vasu, Michael L. (1998). "Fostering Organizational Trust in North Carolina: The Pivotal Role of Administrators and Political Leaders." Administration and Society, March, vol 30, no. 1, p. 62 (23).

Dass, Ram and Gorman, Paul (1985). *How Can I Help?: Stories and Reflections on Service.* New York: Knopf.

Deal, Terrence E. and Hawkins, Pamela C. (1994). Setting the Spirit Free: Tapping Ego Energy from *Managing EGO Energy: The Transformation of Personal Meaning into Organizational Success* (by Ralph Killman). San Francisco: Jossey-Bass.

Foorman, James L. (1997). "Trust and contracts: are they mutually exclusive?" Business & Professional Ethics Journal, spring, vol 16, no 1-3, p. 195.

Fritz, Robert (1991). *Creating.* New York: Fawcett Columbine.

Gardner, M. Robert (1983). *Self Inquiry.* Hillsdale: Analytic Press.

Gawain, Shakti, (1991) *Meditations: Creative Visualization And Meditation Exercises To Enrich Your Life,* San Rafael, Calif. : New World Library.

Georges, Jennifer and Jones, Gareth R. (1998). "The experience and Evolution of Trust: Implications for Cooperation and Teamwork." The Academy of Management Review. July, vol.23, no 3.

Goleman, D. (1995). *Emotional Intelligence*. New York: Bantam.

Hacker, S. K. and DeMarco, J. G. (1995). "Building Community - A Necessary TQ Ingredient." *ASQC 49th Annual Quality Congress Proceedings*, p. 406-412.

Helgesen, Sally (1995). *The Web of Inclusion*. New York: Doubleday.

Katz, Richard (1982). *Boiling Energy: Community Healing among the Kalahari Kung*. Cambridge, MA: Harvard University Press.

Kilmann, Ralph H. (1994). *Managing Ego Energy: The Transformation of Personal Meaning into Organizational Success.* San Francisco: Jossey-Bass.

King, Martin Luther Jr. (1968). "I Have a Dream" The quotations of Martin Luther King Jr. *Compiled and edited by Lotte Hoskins; Grosset & Dunlap, New York Droke House, Publishers, Inc.*

Kohen Daryl, (1997). "Trust and Business: Barriers and Bridges." Business & Professional Ethics Journal, spring, vol 16, no 1-3.

La Porta, Raphael; Lopez-de-Silanes, Florencio; Shleifer, Andrei and Vishny, Robert W. (1997). "Trust in large organization." American Economic Review, May, vol 87, no 2, p. 333.

Li, Tao-Chun (1989). *The Book of Balance and Harmony*. San Francisco: North Point Press.

Luke, Helen M. (1995). *The Way of Woman: Awakening the Perennial Femine*. New York: Doubleday.

Manstead, A.S.R. and Hewstone, Miles (1996). *The Blackwell Encyclopedia of Social Psychology*. Cambridge, MA: Blackwell.

Marciniak, Barbara (1992). *Bringers of the Dawn: Teachings from the Pleiadians*. Santa Fe: Bear & Company, Inc.

McAdams, Dan P. (1993). "The Stories We Live By." Guilford Press.

Mcknight, D. H.; Cummings, L. L. and Chervany, N. L. (1998) "Initial Trust Formation in New Organizational Relationships." The Academy of Management Review, July, vol.23, no 3.

Merton, Thomas (1972). *New Seeds of Contemplation.* New York: New Directions Books.

Neck, Christopher P. and Mlliman, John F. (1994). "Thought Self-Leadership: Finding Spiritual Fulfillment in Organizational Life." *Journal of Managerial Psychology*, vol 9, no 6, p. 9-16.

Peck, M. Scott (1993). *A World Waiting to be Born: Civility Rediscovered.* New York: Bantam.

Peck, M. Scott (1987). *The Different Drum: Community-Making and Peace.* New York: Simon and Schuster.

Rousseau, D. M.; Sitkin, S. B.; Burt, R. S. and Camerer, C. (1998). "Not So Different After All: A Cross Discipline View of Trust." The Academy of Management Review, July, Vol.23, Number 3.

Schlesinger, Leonard A., Eccles, Robert G., and Gabarro, John J. (1983). *Managing Behavior in Organizations: Text, Cases, and Readings.* New York: McGraw-Hill.

Senge, Peter M. (1990). *The Fifth Discipline: The Art and Practice of the Learning Organization.* New York: Doubleday.

Shaw, Robert B. (1997). *Trust in the Balance: Building Successful Organizations on Results, Integrity, and Concerns.* San Francisco: Jossey-Bass.

Sheppard, Blair H. and Sherman, Dana M. (1998). "The Grammar of Trust: A Model and General Implications. *The Academy of Management Review*, July 1998, vol. 23, no 3, 422-437.

Sink, D. Scott and Morris, W.T. (1995). *By What Methods?* Norcross, Georgia: Industrial Engineering & Management Press.

Staub, Robert E. (1996). *The Heart of Leadership: 12 Practices Of Courageous Leaders.* Provo, UT: Executive Excellence Publishing.

Vaill, Peter B. (1989). *Managing as a Performing Art: New Ideas for a World of Chaotic Change.* San Francisco: Jossey-Bass.

Wagner, John (1988). "Spirituality and Administration: The Sign of Integrity." *Weavings: A Journal of the Christian Spiritual Life*, vol 3, no 4, p. 15-16.

Weeks, Dudley (1992). *The Eight Essential Steps to Conflict Resolution: preserving relationships at work, at home, and in the community.* New York, G.P. Putnam's Sons.

Weisbord, Marvin R. (1987). *Productive Workplaces: Organizing and Managing for Dignity, Meaning and Community.* San Francisco, Jossey-Bass Publishers.

Weisbord, Marvin R. (1992). *Discovering Common Ground: How Future Search Conferences Bring People Together to Achieve Breakthrough Innovation, Empowerment, Shared Vision, and Collaborative Action (1st ed.).* San Francisco: Berrett-Koehler.

Williamson, Marianne (1992). *A Return to Love: Reflections on the Principles of A Course in miracles.* New York: Harper Perennial.

Williamson, Marianne (1994). *Illuminata: Thoughts, Prayers, Rites of Passage.* London: Rider.

Zand, Dale E. (1997). *The Leadership Triad.* New York: Oxford University Press.

INDEX

ABOUT THE AUTHORS

Marta C. Wilson, Ph.D., Stephen K. Hacker, and Cindy S. Johnston lead Transformation Systems, a global community of consultants dedicated to the integration of personal, interpersonal, and organizational performance improvement. They also direct The Performance Center, a non-profit learning laboratory affiliated with the Oregon University System and other universities nationwide. The Performance Center conducts action research to help organizations transform knowledge into results.

Marta is a writer and coach who guides development of creation communities within organizations. With a Ph.D. in Industrial and Organizational Psychology from Virginia Tech, Marta has helped numerous leaders achieve desired results over the past ten years. She lives in Virginia with her husband,

Robert. Her next book is a roadmap for intentional living at work, titled *Work Rules*.

Stephen is a motivational speaker, trainer, and organizational consultant with seventeen years of experience at Procter and Gamble. His MBA is from the University of New Orleans. He is a faculty member at Portland State University and lives in Oregon with his wife, Marla, and their children, Jessica and Mark.

Cindy is a partner in Transformation Systems and a senior member of The Performance Center. Her MBA is from Virginia Tech. She is also a contributing author of the book, *By What Method*, by D. Scott Sink and William Morris.

FOR FURTHER INFORMATION

The Performance Center is a non-profit academic and applied learning laboratory, which conducts sponsored action research, training, and public offerings on innovative performance improvement practices.

Transformation Systems integrates personal discovery, interpersonal mastery, and organizational development in order to create comprehensive and sustainable large-scale change.

INFORMATION on these organizations, their products and services, or to order additional copies of *Work Miracles* call **1-888-381-6246** or email **smithsj@performancecenter.org** or visit our web site: **www. performancecenter.org**

ORDER FORM

WORK MIRACLES:
Transform Yourself and Your Organization

Name:

Organization:

Address:

City: State/Zip:

Daytime Phone No.:   E-mail:

Number Ordered ($13.95 each)	
Shipping & Handling *($4.50 for first copy & $1.00 for each additional copy)*	
Sub-total	
Virginia Residents add 4.5% Sales Tax	
Total	

Payment Method *(should be in U.S. Dollars)*

☐ Check *(make payable to:* **Transformation Systems***)*

☐ Visa #:   Expiration date:

☐ MasterCard #:   Expiration date:

Signature:

Credit card orders may be faxed to 540-381-3112
Please mail other orders to: **Transformation Systems**
P.O. Box 11175
Blacksburg, VA 24062-1175
For quantity discounts, please call 1-888-381-6246

INSIGHT PRESS™